ROSE ELLIOT
THE
CLASSIC
VEGETARIAN
COOKBOOK

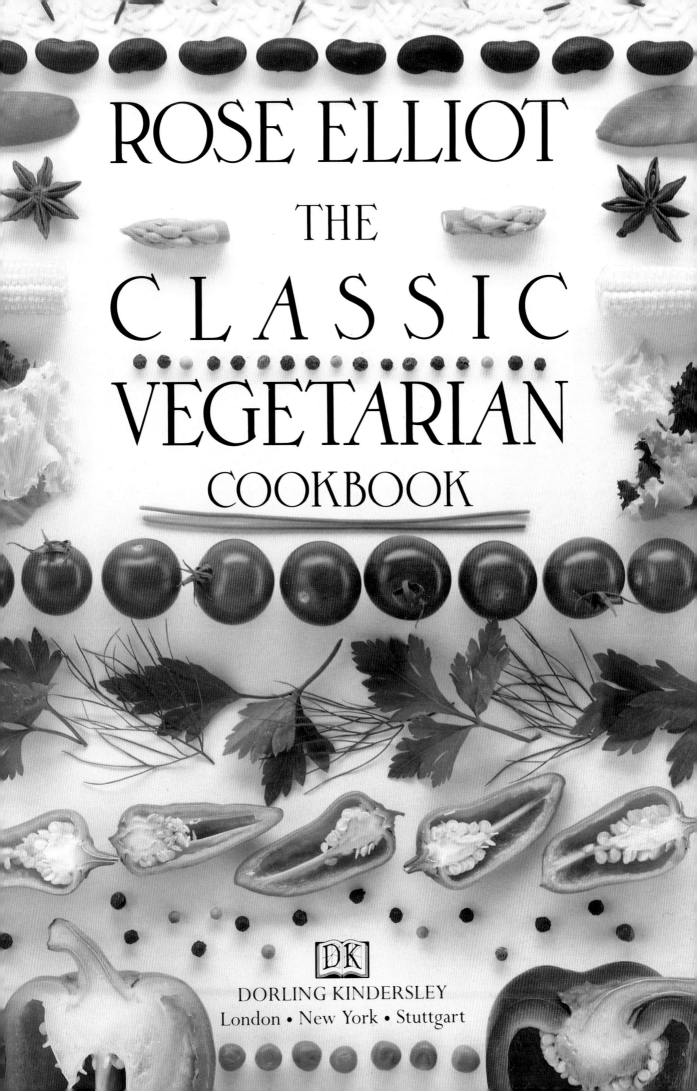

ROSE ELLIOT

THE

CLASSIC

VEGETARIAN

COOKBOOK

DK

DORLING KINDERSLEY

London • New York • Stuttgart

A DORLING KINDERSLEY BOOK

Project Editor
Mari Roberts

Art Editor
Tracey Clarke

Designer
Kate Scott

Managing Editor
Rosie Pearson

Managing Art Editor
Carole Ash

US Editors
Jeanette Mall, Julee Binder, Frances Cleary

Photography
Clive Streeter
Amanda Heywood

Senior Production Manager
Maryann Rogers

*To vegetarians, and would-be vegetarians,
with love*

First American Edition, 1994
2 4 6 8 10 9 7 5 3 1

Published in the United States by
Dorling Kindersley Publishing, Inc., 95 Madison Avenue
New York, NY 10016

Published in Great Britain by Dorling Kindersley Limited

Distributed by Houghton Mifflin Company, Boston

LIBRARY OF CONGRESS CATALOGING-IN-PUBLICATION DATA

Elliot, Rose.
    The classic vegetarian cookbook / by Rose Elliot. -- 1st American ed.
    p. cm.
    Includes index.
    ISBN 1-56458-486-0
    1. Cookery, vegetarian I. Title

TX837.E397   1994
641.5'636--dc20   93-6085
                                                      CIP

Reproduced in Thailand by J. Film Process Co., Ltd.
Printed and bound in Italy by A. Mondadori, Verona

CONTENTS

INTRODUCTION 6

CLASSIC DISHES

*A unique photographic catalog featuring
ten key classic vegetarian dishes
with ingredients and recipe variations*

RECIPES

A wide range of recipes, influenced by cuisines from around the world, for every occasion from quick meals to special celebrations

TECHNIQUES

Step-by-step preparation and cooking techniques

INTRODUCTION

When I was about three I first made the connection between the fish that my mother was preparing for supper and the fish that swim in the sea. I made a fuss, which I can still remember, and refused to eat my meal. That is when I became vegetarian.

Another trait that surfaced early was a love of cooking. My mother tells stories of my early experiments in the kitchen as a child, when my use of ingredients was lavish, and the piles of washing up immense. My parents' tolerance paid off. They ran a retreat center, and the skills that I acquired enabled me to take over the cooking there when I was in my late teens. There were few vegetarian recipes to guide me, so I frequently experimented. Guests constantly asked for my recipes and so, audaciously and rather innocently at such a young age, I wrote my first cookbook, *Simply Delicious*, which was published in 1967. This was one of the first exclusively vegetarian cookbooks published in the UK and its success led to more – in fact, I didn't stop writing and have now produced over forty books.

Over the years my style of cooking, although always vegetarian, has changed and developed greatly, as an ever-increasing range of ingredients has become available and as I've traveled, learned, and continued to experiment. The emphasis on straightforward dishes that are fairly quick and undemanding to make has, however, remained. This is partly because of my circumstances – with home, family, and career to manage – and partly because simple fresh food, with all the flavor of the natural ingredients intact, is my preference.

The many recipes I have selected and created for this book fall into two main categories: long-established, traditional recipes and innovative new ones. You will find the best of classic vegetarian cuisine here, such as delectable fondue, creamy gratin dauphinois and colorful, crunchy salads, together with fresh ideas for vegetable terrines and roulades, delicate crêpes and melting pastries. Even though desserts need not be designated "vegetarian," I don't believe a cookbook is complete without them, and so here you will find recipes ranging from chocolate brownies to a rose-petal sorbet.

I have given suggestions for creating meals from these recipes in the menu planning section, and you will find they cover most occasions, from casual, loosely structured suppers to formal dinners. Whether you are fully vegetarian or demi-vegetarian, or simply want to make delicious meals for vegetarian friends and family, I hope that you will take pleasure in reading this book, using the recipes, and enjoying the results.

Rose Elliot

CLASSIC DISHES

*The ten classic dishes featured here represent
the best of the world's vegetarian cuisine. From
a light savory strudel to a Thai-style stir-fry, a
vegetable terrine to a golden cheese soufflé,
these dishes and their variations provide a preview
of the recipes that come later in the book
and an overview of how exciting
vegetarian cooking can be.*

TERRINES

Colorful and eye-catching, vegetable terrines are a modern vegetarian classic. They are simple to make, delicious, and versatile. A terrine may be served as a starter or as a light main course, and many are good hot or cold. This beautiful, fragrant terrine is perfect for a celebratory summer meal; it serves 6 as a starter.

TOMATO, ZUCCHINI, RED PEPPER, & BASIL

INGREDIENTS

butter and grated Parmesan to coat the pan
1 tbsp olive oil
1 medium-sized onion, chopped
1 clove garlic, chopped
14oz can whole peeled tomatoes,
coarsely chopped, with juice
2 medium-sized zucchini, cut into thin slices
2 red peppers, quartered
3 tbsps light cream
2 tbsps freshly grated Parmesan cheese
1 tbsp tomato purée, preferably sundried
3 eggs, beaten
salt and freshly ground black pepper
bunch of fresh basil, including some sprigs to garnish

PREPARATION

1 Preheat the oven to 325°F/160°C. Line a 3 x 5 x 9-inch loaf pan with waxed paper, grease lightly with butter, and dust with Parmesan.
2 Heat the oil in a saucepan over moderate heat, add the onion, cover, and cook for 5 minutes. Add the garlic and cook for another minute.
3 Pour in the tomatoes together with their juice. Reduce the heat and simmer, uncovered, until the liquid has evaporated and the mixture reduced, about 15 minutes. Remove from the heat.
4 Boil the zucchini until tender, drain, refresh under cold water, and pat dry with paper towels.
5 Roast and peel the peppers as shown on page 144. Remove the stalk and seeds, and cut into strips.
6 Stir the cream, Parmesan, tomato purée, and eggs into the tomato mixture. Season well.
7 Fill the pan in layers: some tomato mixture, the zucchini, more tomato, the basil leaves, and the strips of red pepper with the last of the tomato.
8 Bake the terrine in a bain-marie (see page 147) in the oven until set and firm: about 1¼ hours. Cool before removing from the pan.

Red pepper

Zucchini

Canned tomatoes

Garlic

Onion

Olive oil

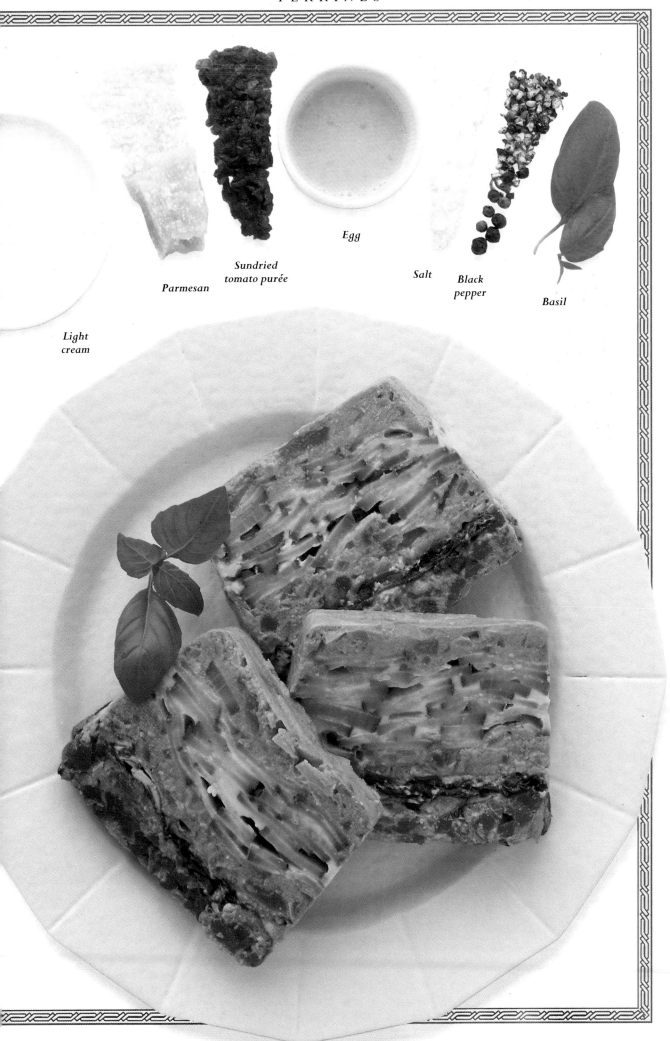

Light
cream

Parmesan

Sundried
tomato purée

Egg

Salt

Black
pepper

Basil

A SELECTION OF TERRINES

VEGETABLES IN A SPINACH COAT

Layers of rich-tasting artichoke heart, asparagus, and sundried tomato are set in a cottage cheese and chives mixture and wrapped in spinach leaves. The sauce is made from sundried tomatoes (page 121).

See page 67 for recipe.

PUMPKIN, BROCCOLI, & LEEK

This is a good terrine for autumn or winter, making the most of the colors of puréed and sliced pumpkin, which contrast with the broccoli and leek. Green pepper sauce (page 120), shown here, is an excellent accompaniment, as is mayonnaise mixed with thick yogurt. Garnish with chervil.

See page 69 for recipe.

STRIPED VEGETABLE

Bright stripes of carrot, broad bean, and turnip, layered with chervil, make this a stunning opening to a meal, and fresh tomato sauce (page 121) is a dramatic addition. You can use other vegetables in the terrine according to the season, aiming for contrasting colors and tastes.

See page 68 for recipe.

PEPPERS & BABY CORN COBS

Mediterranean flavors and bright colors make this a favorite summer terrine for the first course of a light salad meal. A thin pesto sauce (page 123) and a basil garnish set it off well, in both color and flavor.

See page 66 for recipe.

GREEN PEA, MINT, & CAULIFLOWER

This is a refreshing, summery dish, perfect with thick yogurt brightened up by a little saffron, as here, or with a warm hollandaise sauce (page 123). The clean taste of the mint is complemented by the sweetness of the peas and the mildness of the cauliflower.

See page 67 for recipe.

LENTIL, CARROT, & FENNEL

A light lentil mixture flavored with turmeric and mixed with carrot, fennel, and flat-leaf parsley makes this unusual terrine. It is delicious cold, either as a starter or as part of a buffet. Here it is served with red pepper sauce (page 120) and garnished with dill.

See page 68 for recipe.

OMELETTES

A classic omelette – folded, and slightly runny inside – is quick and easy to make, and delicious at any time of the day. The technique is simple, and success depends largely on having a frying pan of the right size: if it is too big for the number of eggs, the omelette will be thin and tough; if too small, it will be spongy and thick. Omelettes are versatile, too. You can fill them with a wide choice of ingredients, such as mushrooms, ratatouille, or for a particular treat, shavings of black truffle. This is a two-egg omelette, ideal for one person, cooked in a 6-inch frying pan, with the simple addition of fragrant chopped fresh herbs stirred into the eggs before they are cooked.

Egg

Salt

Black pepper

Flat-leaf parsley

FRESH HERB OMELETTE

INGREDIENTS

2 eggs
salt and freshly ground black pepper
2 tsps finely chopped fresh flat-leaf parsley
1 tsp finely chopped fresh chives
1 tsp finely chopped fresh chervil
1 tsp finely chopped fresh tarragon
1 tbsp butter

PREPARATION

1 Break the eggs into a bowl and beat them lightly until the whites and yolks have just combined. Season with salt and black pepper. Add the herbs.
2 Place a small frying pan (6 inches across the base) over moderate heat and, when it is hot, put in the butter, turn the heat up to high, and swirl the butter around the pan without letting it brown.
3 Pour in the eggs, tipping the pan so that it is evenly coated. Using a fork, gently draw the edges of the egg toward the center and let the liquid egg run to the edges. Keep doing this until the omelette is almost set but still a little moist on top – it takes around a minute.
4 To serve the omelette folded in half as shown here, hold the pan over a warmed plate and slide the omelette onto the plate, allowing the top half to flip over and cover the bottom half on the plate. Alternatively, fold it in three. While the omelette is still in the pan, flip one third over toward the center, then slide it onto a warmed plate, unfolded edge first, allowing the folded part to flip over and cover the rest. (See page 148 for an illustration of this method.)
5 Serve and eat at once.

Chives

Chervil

Tarragon

Butter

PHYLLO PIES & PARCELS

Crisp and golden phyllo parcels and strudels, filled with moist and tender vegetables, are delicious and surprisingly easy to make. Thin sheets of ready-made phyllo pastry can be used for elaborate main dishes, such as the sliced strudel shown here, or for simple but original snacks (see overleaf). Ingredients may be varied to suit the occasion. For example, make the vegetable strudel with parsnips and blue cheese instead of the Swiss chard, and replace the olives with pinenuts. This strudel serves 6.

VEGETABLE STRUDEL

INGREDIENTS

*5 cups Swiss chard, leaves and stems separated
and roughly torn
4 carrots, cut into sticks
1⅔ cups cooked artichoke bottoms (page 146), sliced
2 egg yolks
⅔ cup light cream
2 tbsps finely chopped fresh flat-leaf parsley
salt and freshly ground black pepper
1 packet of phyllo pastry and melted butter for brushing
⅓ cup black olives, pitted and sliced*

PREPARATION

1 Preheat the oven to 400°F/200°C.

2 Cook the Swiss chard leaves until tender in just the water that clings to them after washing. Cook the Swiss chard stems and the carrots separately in a little boiling water until tender. Drain.

3 Put the vegetables into a big bowl with the artichokes, egg yolks, cream, and parsley. Combine well. Season to taste with salt and pepper.

4 Spread a clean dish cloth on the work surface and place on it two or four sheets of phyllo pastry (depending on their size), side by side, over-lapping ½ inch to make a rectangle about 18 x 20 inches. Brush all over with melted butter. Make another rectangle of the same size on top of the first and brush with butter again.

5 Spread the filling evenly over the phyllo to within 1 inch of the edges. Sprinkle the olives on top. Turn over the edges to make a "hem," then roll up the strudel firmly from one of the long edges. Brush it all over with melted butter. For extra flakiness, wrap one or two more sheets of phyllo around the strudel, brushing with butter.

6 Place the strudel on a baking sheet, curving it into a half moon. Bake until crisp and golden brown: about 35 minutes. Serve at once, or recrisp later by returning it briefly to a hot oven.

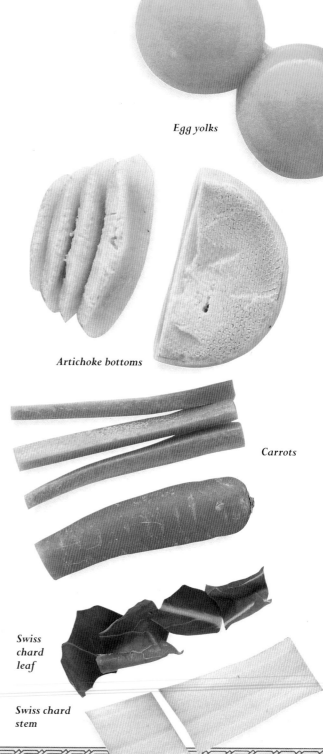

Egg yolks

Artichoke bottoms

Carrots

Swiss chard leaf

Swiss chard stem

Light cream

Flat-leaf parsley

Salt

Black pepper

Phyllo pastry brushed with butter

Olives

PHYLLO SHAPES & PARCELS

LITTLE GREEK PIES

Bite-size versions of a classic Greek pie, these crisp triangles contain a mixture of salty feta cheese, spinach enlivened by fennel seeds, and a little onion. They make an excellent snack, hot or cold.

See page 110 for recipe.

PHYLLO FLOWERS

Small squares of phyllo pastry arranged into flower shapes make pretty containers for mouthwatering asparagus with hollandaise sauce. Other vegetables work well too, such as broccoli with strips of tomato. The flowers can be made in advance, but fill them at the last minute so they stay crisp.

See page 109 for recipe.

SPRING ROLLS

Phyllo is perfect for spring rolls, which can be deep-fried or, as here, brushed with oil, sprinkled with sesame seeds, and baked. The filling is a Chinese-style mixture of peppers, bean sprouts, and mushrooms.

See page 109 for recipe.

LEEK PARCELS

These light phyllo parcels are filled with a creamy leek mixture. To hint at the filling, serve the parcels "tied up" with a leek ribbon. Tying up is easier if the raw leek is first dipped in hot water to soften it.

See page 109 for recipe.

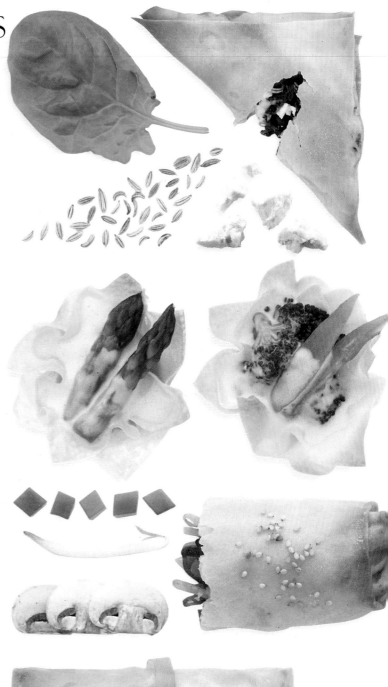

MONEY BAGS

The combination of crisp pastry with a filling of smooth ricotta and flavorful Parmesan is delicious. Other possible fillings are spinach and feta (as in the Little Greek Pies), ratatouille, or fried mushrooms. Serve the phyllo Money Bags as a first course or a snack.

See page 110 for recipe.

Asparagus phyllo flowers

Phyllo flowers with broccoli and tomato

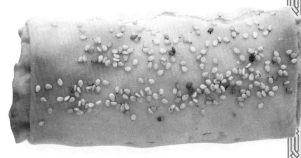

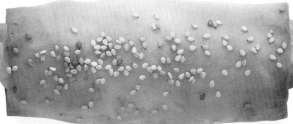

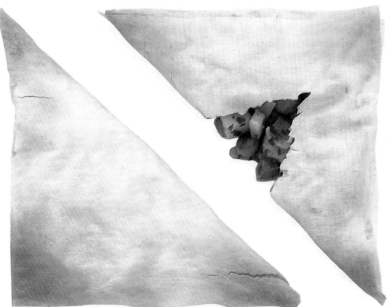

SPICED VEGETABLE TRIANGLES

These triangles are filled with a lightly spiced mixture of vegetables. They make a good starter for an Indian meal, and are also popular eaten on their own as a snack.

See page 110 for recipe.

PASTA

Springtime pasta, or Pasta Primavera, is a classic Italian dish, full of fresh spring vegetables and herbs. You can use any tender young vegetables: zucchini, asparagus, and baby carrots are delicious options. The trick with pasta is to bite a piece as it boils to ensure you don't pass the stage known to Italians as *al dente*, where the pasta still offers some resistance to the teeth. Pasta Primavera serves 4 as a first course, 2 as a main course.

PASTA PRIMAVERA

INGREDIENTS

1¼ cups shelled broad beans
2 tbsps butter
1 cup green beans, trimmed
1 cup snow peas, trimmed
½lb fettuccine or linguine
2 tbsps chopped fresh flat-leaf parsley
1 tbsp chopped fresh dill
1 tbsp chopped fresh chives
salt and freshly ground black pepper

PREPARATION

1 Cook the broad beans in a little boiling water until just tender: about 2 minutes. Drain, allow to cool, then pop out of their skins using your finger and thumb. Put them into a medium-sized saucepan along with the butter and set aside.
2 Pour 2 quarts of water into a large pan and place over high heat. This is for the pasta.
3 Put the green beans in a small pan, cover with boiling water and cook until tender: 3–4 minutes. Drain and add to the pan with the broad beans.
4 Put the snow peas in the small pan, cover with boiling water and cook for 1 minute. Drain and add to the other vegetables. Place over gentle heat and warm the vegetables in the butter.
5 When the water for the pasta reaches a rolling boil, drop the pasta in. Allow the water to come back to a boil, give the pasta a quick stir, then let the water boil steadily until the pasta is tender but still offers some resistance to the teeth: bite a piece to find out. Pasta cooks in a few minutes.
6 Drain the pasta but leave some water clinging to it, and put it back into the hot pan. Add the warm vegetables with their butter, and the herbs. Toss well, season to taste with salt and black pepper, and toss again, making sure the pasta is well coated. Serve at once.

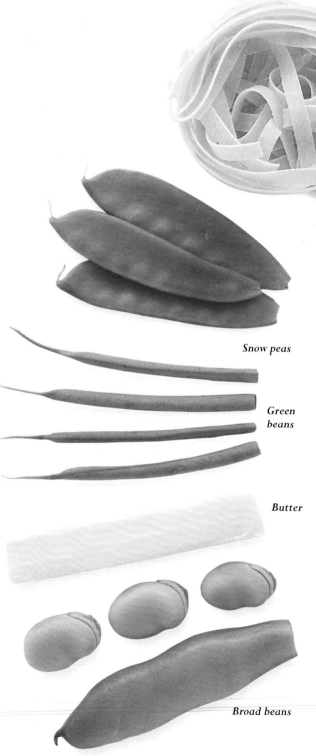

Snow peas

Green beans

Butter

Broad beans

Dill

Chives

Salt

Black
pepper

Flat-leaf
parsley

Fettuccine

STUFFED VEGETABLES

Many vegetables lend themselves to being filled, and the ingredients you can use are varied and versatile. Stuffed vegetables make compact, tasty snacks for a picnic, and can grace a dinner table, too. Artichokes, in particular, make a stunning first course. This recipe serves 4 as a starter, allowing one artichoke per person.

TOMATO-FILLED ARTICHOKES

INGREDIENTS

4 large globe artichokes, stalks and leaf points removed
½ lemon

THE FILLING

1 tbsp olive oil
1 small onion, chopped
1 clove garlic, chopped
14oz can whole peeled tomatoes,
coarsely chopped, with juice
salt and freshly ground black pepper
8 fresh basil leaves, roughly torn
fresh chives, to garnish

PREPARATION

1 Make sure the bases of the prepared artichokes are level, then rub all the cut surfaces with the lemon to preserve the color. Fill a saucepan large enough to hold the artichokes (or two that will each hold two) with water and bring to a boil.

2 Put the artichokes into the boiling water and cover with a small plate to keep them submerged. Let them simmer for about 30 minutes or until you can easily pull a leaf from one of them. Drain them upside down in a colander or on a wire rack.

3 Preheat the oven to 350°F/180°C.

4 To make the filling, warm the oil in a saucepan over moderate heat, add the onion, cover, and cook for 5 minutes. Add the garlic and cook for another 1–2 minutes. Pour in the tomatoes with their juice and cook, uncovered, until the mixture has reduced: about 15 minutes. Remove from the heat, season to taste, and add the basil.

5 Take the artichokes and pull out the pale inner leaves, then use a teaspoon to scoop out the fluffy choke. Spoon the tomato filling into the hollow that is left. Place in a shallow casserole dish, cover with foil, and bake in the preheated oven until heated through: about 20 minutes.

6 Serve on warmed plates with chopped chives sprinkled on top. To eat, tear off the leaves one by one and dip the fleshy, edible part in the filling. Work your way down to the base, and eat that too.

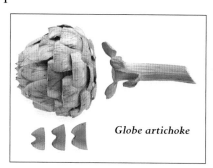

Globe artichoke

Lemon

Olive oil

Onion

Garlic

Canned tomatoes

Salt

Black
pepper

Basil

Chives

23

STUFFED VEGETABLES

CHILI LIME AVOCADOS

These avocados are stuffed with a mixture of onion, garlic, chili, chives, and lime, and baked just long enough to heat through — if they are cooked for longer, their flavor is spoiled. Garnish with slices of lime and any fresh herb that is available; here it is cilantro.

See page 63 for recipe.

BABY EGGPLANTS WITH MUSHROOMS & NUTS

Tomatoes and parsley are combined with mushrooms and pinenuts to make the stuffing for these attractive baby eggplants. You can use larger eggplants if the baby ones are unavailable, or if you lack the time to prepare the more difficult smaller ones. Stuffed eggplants are delicious both hot and cold.

See page 64 for recipe.

PEPPERS WITH ROASTED VEGETABLES

This is an eye-catching way to serve roasted vegetables — and it's easy to do because you roast the peppers and all the vegetables together. Basil is used here to garnish.

See page 65 for recipe.

HERBY TOMATOES

Thyme combined with bread crumbs, olive oil, and flat-leaf parsley (which can also be a garnish) makes a fragrant stuffing for a large tomato. This is an ideal summer dish when tomatoes and herbs are plentiful and at their best. The flavor always transports me straight to Provence.

See page 65 for recipe.

CREAM CHEESE MUSHROOMS

For a simple yet flavorful stuffing for mushrooms, use cream cheese with herbs and garlic. Small or large mushrooms may be used but they should be as open and flat as possible. Lemon strips (page 145) and dill make a delicate garnish.

See page 65 for recipe.

ZUCCHINI WITH ALMONDS & RED PEPPER

This is a particularly good mix of flavors, colors, and textures. Yellow peppers may be used instead of red, and pinenuts or pistachios instead of almonds. Fresh thyme is added to the filling, and here thyme is also the garnish.

See page 63 for recipe.

SOUFFLES

Served the instant it comes out of the oven, a soufflé is one of the most impressive dishes you can make. The timing is crucial but the preparation is easy, and much can be done in advance. It is important to use the right-sized soufflé dish so that when the mixture expands, it does not overflow onto the oven floor. This delicious golden soufflé, garnished with edible flowers, serves 3 people as a generous main course.

FOUR-CHEESE SOUFFLE

INGREDIENTS

2 tbsps butter, plus extra to grease the dish
¼ cup all-purpose flour
1⅓ cups milk
5 egg whites, 4 egg yolks
½ cup Parmesan cheese, grated
⅓ cup Gruyère cheese, grated
¼ cup blue cheese, crumbled
¼ cup mozzarella cheese, diced
salt and freshly ground black pepper
edible flowers such as nasturtiums, to garnish

Parmesan

PREPARATION

1 Melt the butter and stir in the flour, then slowly add the milk to make a béchamel sauce, as shown on page 148. Simmer over very gentle heat for 10 minutes, then allow to cool slightly.
2 Stir the four egg yolks (save the fifth to use in another recipe) and all the cheeses into the sauce and season to taste. Transfer to a bowl.

Egg yolks

 You can prepare ahead up to this point. The cheese mixture and the egg whites keep for several hours, covered, in the refrigerator.

3 Preheat the oven to 400°F/200°C. Butter a 9-inch soufflé dish and tie a piece of buttered waxed paper around the outside extending at least 2 inches above the rim.
4 In a clean bowl, whisk the five egg whites until they are stiff. Stir a quarter of the egg whites into the soufflé mixture to loosen it, then gently fold in the rest, using a metal spoon.

Milk

5 Pour the mixture into the dish. To make the soufflé rise in a top-hat shape, draw the handle of a wooden spoon through its surface in a circle.
6 Bake until the soufflé is risen and golden brown: about 25 minutes. Serve immediately.

All-purpose flour

Butter

Gruyère

Blue cheese

Mozzarella

Salt

Black
pepper

Egg white

Nasturtium

QUICHES & TARTS

My way of cooking a classic savory quiche is to "waterproof" the pastry case with hot oil and to pre-cook the custard. The result is a crisp case with a light filling. This recipe makes four individual quiches, each with tender broccoli and creamy Brie in a light savory custard.

BROCCOLI & BRIE QUICHES

INGREDIENTS

THE PASTRY

4-inch pastry shells
(pages 150–1), uncooked
2 tbsps olive oil
1 shallot, chopped
1 clove garlic, chopped

THE FILLING

1¼ cups broccoli florets
3 egg yolks, 2 egg whites
1¼ cups light cream
salt and freshly ground black pepper
freshly grated nutmeg
¼lb Brie, thinly sliced
2 tbsps freshly grated Parmesan cheese
1–2 tbsps pinenuts

PREPARATION

1 Preheat the oven to 400°F/200°C.

2 Prepare and bake the pastry shells as described on pages 150-1. About 5 minutes before they are done, heat the oil in a saucepan and fry the shallot and garlic until golden. As soon as the shells come out of the oven, pour the hot oil into them, letting it run over the pastry to waterproof and flavor it.

3 Turn the oven down to 325°F/160°C.

4 Half-boil, half-steam the broccoli in a little water until barely tender: about 3–4 minutes. Drain, refresh with cold running water, and dry in a colander.

5 To make the custard, break the eggs into a small bowl, pour in the cream; mix well. Pour the mixture into a saucepan and stir over low heat until it begins to coat the back of the spoon. Remove from the heat, season with salt, pepper, and nutmeg, and stir in half the Parmesan.

6 Arrange the Brie and the broccoli in the base of each quiche and pour the custard over them. Sprinkle the rest of the Parmesan and the pinenuts on top. Bake until the filling is set and golden brown: 20–25 minutes. Serve hot, warm, or cold.

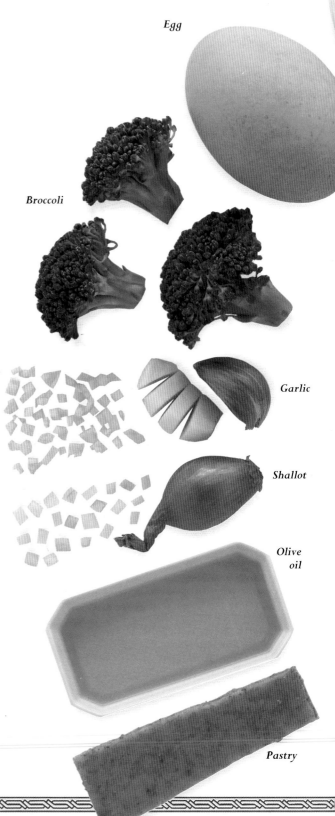

Egg

Broccoli

Garlic

Shallot

Olive oil

Pastry

Light cream

Salt

Black pepper

Nutmeg

Brie

Parmesan

Pinenuts

QUICHES & TARTLETS

CHERRY TOMATO BARQUETTES

In these boat-shaped tartlets, cherry tomatoes are baked in a light custard. The shells may be prebaked or not, as you prefer, but the pastry must be thin.

See page 105 for recipe.

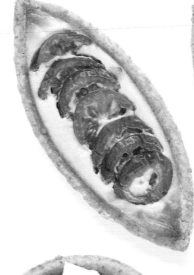

Black olive and tomato   **Feta, arugula, and sundried tomato**

LEEK & SESAME QUICHE

The mixture of creamy leeks with sesame seed pastry is unusual and delicious. The pastry shell should be prebaked and "waterproofed" with hot oil as described on pages 150-1 to make it beautifully crisp.

See page 105 for recipe.

SMALL QUICHES

Mini versions of quiches can be filled with unusual ingredients for originality. Small avocado and scallion quiches are complemented well by fragrant carrot and cardamom ones, and together they are excellent as part of a party spread.

See page 105 for recipe.

Avocado and scallion   **Carrot and cardamom**

MIXED PEPPER BARQUETTES

Crisp prebaked shells are given a moist and juicy filling of strips of red and yellow pepper. Basil leaves make an attractive garnish as well as adding to the scent and flavor of the barquettes.

See page 105 for recipe.

MEDITERRANEAN TARTLETS

Prebaked tartlets full of Mediterranean flavors: a thick tomato mixture with black olives, and diced feta cheese with arugula and sundried tomatoes. They make an excellent first course or party snack.

See page 105 for recipes.

BLUE CHEESE & ONION QUICHE WITH ALMONDS

Blue cheese gives this quiche a distinctive tangy flavor, with which sweet-tasting crunchy almonds contrast well. You could, however, use another cheese instead, such as sharp Cheddar for a smoother flavor.

See page 105 for recipe.

STIR-FRIES

The classic Eastern way of cooking fresh vegetables is to chop them finely and fry them quickly and vigorously in hot, fragrant oil. It is a healthy method, cooking the vegetables so fast that they retain their individual tastes and firm texture. For a successful stir-fry, it is important to prepare all the ingredients before you start to cook, get the oil smoking hot before you add them, and cook them briefly, stirring continuously. Served with rice, a stir-fry makes a complete main course. This stir-fry is Thai-style with lemongrass, star anise, chili, lime, fresh cilantro, and soy sauce. You can use all or some of these flavorings, according to taste and availability. This recipe serves 4.

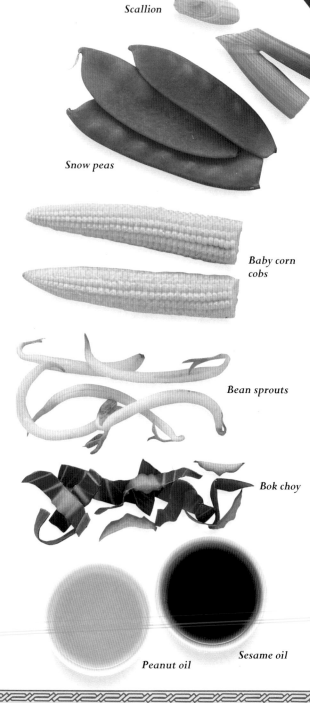

Scallion

Snow peas

Baby corn cobs

Bean sprouts

Bok choy

Peanut oil

Sesame oil

THAI-STYLE STIR-FRY VEGETABLES

INGREDIENTS

1 tbsp sesame oil
1 tbsp peanut oil
1 small bok choy, shredded
1 cup bean sprouts
1 cup baby corn cobs
½ cup snow peas, trimmed
small bunch of scallions, chopped
1 red pepper, cored, seeded, and thinly sliced
1 cup button mushrooms, sliced, or straw mushrooms
(from a jar or can), kept whole
1 stalk of lemongrass, white part finely sliced
1 fresh green chili, seeded, and finely chopped
1 or 2 whole pods of star anise, seeds removed
and crushed
1 tbsp soy sauce
juice and finely grated zest of 1 lime
2 – 3 tbsps chopped fresh cilantro

PREPARATION

1 Pour the oils into a wok or a large frying pan and place over high heat.
2 When the oils are smoking hot, drop in all the vegetables, the white part of the lemongrass, the chili, and the star anise seeds. As the vegetables fry, stir them vigorously with a long-handled wooden spoon until they are evenly heated through but still crisp: about 2 minutes.
3 Put in the soy sauce, lime juice and zest, and cilantro all at once. Stir again over the heat, allowing the mixture to sizzle for just a few seconds. Serve immediately.

Lime juice

Star anise

Soy sauce

Lime zest

Chili

Lemongrass

Cilantro

Mushrooms

Red pepper

ROULADES

Slices of roulade, with their vivid spirals, make an impressive dish for a special meal. Most roulades gain texture and flavor from a semi-hard cheese, such as Gruyère, and are lightened by eggs. Variations include spinach or cashews; and one of the stunning roulades overleaf is an egg-free and cheese-free version made with red beans. The roulade here serves 6 as a starter, with fresh tomato sauce (page 121).

GRUYERE & HERB ROULADE WITH ASPARAGUS

INGREDIENTS

butter and grated Parmesan to coat the pan
¾ cup cottage cheese
⅔ cup light cream
4 eggs, separated
1¾ cups Gruyère cheese, grated
3 tbsps chopped fresh herbs: chervil, flat-leaf parsley
salt and freshly ground black pepper
1½ cups asparagus tips

PREPARATION

1 Preheat the oven to 400°F/200°C. Line a 9 x 13-inch shallow-sided baking pan with waxed paper, butter it, and dust with the Parmesan.
2 Put one third of the cottage cheese into a large bowl, add the cream, and mix until smooth. Beat in the egg yolks, one by one. Finally, stir in the Gruyère cheese and the herbs, and season to taste.
3 In a separate bowl, whisk the egg whites until they are stiff. Fold gently into the cheese mixture using a metal spoon. Pour this mixture into the prepared baking pan, smoothing it to the edges, and bake until risen and just firm in the center: about 12–15 minutes.
4 Take the roulade out of the oven and turn it out, face down, onto waxed paper sprinkled with a little Parmesan. Peel the paper from the top.
5 Prepare the filling. Wash the asparagus well, break off and discard the tough stalk ends, then boil or steam until tender: about 4–7 minutes.
6 Soften the remaining cottage cheese with about 2 tablespoons of water. Spread mixture over the roulade. Arrange the asparagus on top in rows, lining them up with the short side of the roulade. Roll up the roulade, as shown on page 95.
7 Serve at once, cut into slices, or reheat wrapped in aluminum foil in a 325°F/180°C oven, for approximately 15 minutes.

Gruyère

Egg yolks

Light cream

Cottage cheese

Flat-leaf parsley

Chervil

Egg whites

Salt

Black pepper

Asparagus tips

A SELECTION OF ROULADES

GRUYERE WITH RED PEPPERS

Sweet-tasting roasted red pepper makes a good filling for a Gruyère roulade and provides a bright color contrast. Quick herb sauce (page 123), made with chives, goes well. Garnish with oregano.

See page 94 for recipe.

SPINACH WITH CREAM CHEESE & RED PEPPER

Here a roulade of spinach is spread with cream cheese and irregularly placed strips of roasted red pepper. The color and flavor of yellow pepper sauce (page 120) makes it the perfect accompaniment, and basil is a fragrant garnish.

See page 96 for recipe.

GRUYERE & HERBS WITH ARUGULA & AVOCADO

Peppery arugula contrasts well with the creamy-tasting avocado spread in this roulade. Other green leaves, such as watercress and mâche, are excellent alternatives. Serve cold, with fresh tomato sauce (page 121), and garnish with arugula.

See page 94 for recipe.

RED BEAN ROULADE

The texture of this unusual roulade is softer than most. Serve it in slices on individual plates, rather than transferred whole to a serving dish, and gently reshape the slices using a palette knife. It is delicious served with an avocado sauce (page 123) and garnished with cilantro.

See page 116 for recipe.

CHEDDAR & HERBS WITH MUSHROOMS

Red wine sauce (page 121) complements this roulade well, and also makes it ideal for serving on a festive occasion such as Christmas. Any sort of mushroom can be used in the filling. Garnish with thyme.

See page 94 for recipe.

CASHEW WITH BROCCOLI

This is a very rich roulade for a special occasion. Serve it with hollandaise sauce (page 123) and garnish simply with flat-leaf parsley. Pecans or really fresh walnuts (be careful to choose ones with no hint of bitterness) can be used instead of the cashews. For a lighter dish, serve with crème fraîche or plain yogurt.

See page 96 for recipe.

CREPES

Light and delicious, crêpes can be layered, rolled, or folded and filled with a wide variety of ingredients. Here crêpe cones are stuffed with leek and tarragon cream. Serves 4.

CREAMY LEEK & TARRAGON CREPES

INGREDIENTS

1 quantity of crêpe batter (page 149)
olive oil for cooking the crêpes
1lb trimmed leeks, sliced
1¼ cups crème fraîche
1 tbsp chopped fresh flat-leaf parsley
2 tbsps chopped fresh tarragon
salt and freshly ground black pepper

PREPARATION

1 Preheat the oven to 350°F/180°C so that you can keep the crêpes warm once they are done. Place the batter and a ladle next to the stove.
2 Heat a small frying pan (6 inches across the base) and brush with olive oil. When the oil is hot enough to sizzle when a drop of water is dropped into it, take the pan off the heat and, using the ladle, pour in enough of the batter – 2 tablespoons – to coat the base. Return the pan to the heat and let the crêpe cook until the top is set and lightly browned: about 1 minute. Flip it over by tossing it or turning it with a palette knife and your fingers.
3 Cook the second side until lightly browned, just a few seconds. Lift the crêpe out of the pan onto a piece of foil. Reheat the pan – you won't need to regrease it every time – and make the rest of the crêpes in the same way, stacking them up on foil. Cover with more foil and keep warm in the oven.

 You can prepare the crêpes ahead of time. Wrap in foil and keep in the refrigerator for up to 3 days, or in the freezer for up to 3 months.

4 Cover the leeks with boiling water and cook until they are just tender: about 5–7 minutes. Drain.
5 Put the leeks into a saucepan with the crème fraîche. Bring to a boil, reduce the heat and let the crème fraîche bubble away until it has reduced to a thick sauce and the leeks are tender: about 10 minutes. Stir in the herbs and season to taste.
6 Remove the warmed crêpes from the oven. Fold each one in half, then into quarters, spoon the filling under the top fold and serve.

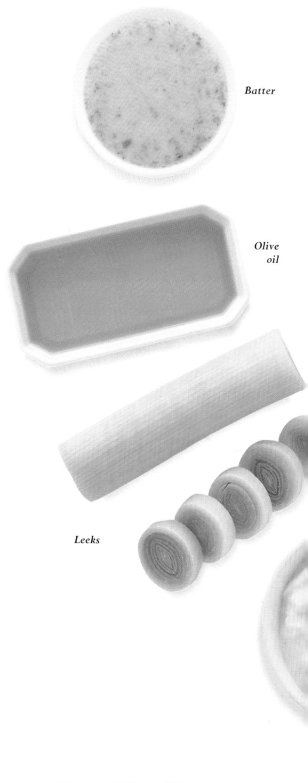

Batter

Olive oil

Leeks

Crème fraîche

Flat-leaf parsley

Tarragon

Salt

Black
pepper

RECIPES

This wonderfully eclectic collection is drawn from many different food cultures, proving that vegetarian cooking is truly international. Never again will anyone be able to say that vegetarian food is dull, after sampling such delights as tempura, gazpacho, couscous, falafel, and spiced okra. Classic French dishes are well represented too, with soufflés, roulades, crêpes, and terrines. One of the pleasures of vegetarian cooking is that dishes are flexible, they can play any part in a meal, from supporting role to main lead. To make life easier the menu planning section offers ideas for all sorts of occasions, from quick and easy suppers to formal dinner parties.

SOUPS

Soups are less complicated to make than many people imagine; some of the best classic soups are simply vegetables cooked gently in a little butter or olive oil, then simmered in water or stock until tender, and sieved, mashed, or puréed. Cream and chopped fresh herbs add a special touch. It is easy to make flavorful vegetable stock, which freezes well, but even if you have none, don't be put off making soups: They can taste very good when made with just water, allowing the clear natural flavors to come through.

VEGETABLE STOCK

Make a habit of saving the water in which vegetables are cooked, and you will have a constant supply of excellent stock. To make stock from scratch, however, use odds and ends of vegetables, as here. Makes about 1 quart.

INGREDIENTS

2lb mixed vegetables, such as onions, celery, carrot trimmings, leek trimmings, parsley stalks
several cloves garlic, unpeeled
2 bay leaves
1 tbsp black peppercorns
1 or 2 sprigs of thyme
strip of lemon zest, optional

PREPARATION

1 Put all the ingredients into a large saucepan or pot, cover with about 6 cups of water, bring to a boil, then cover, and leave to simmer until the vegetables are soft: 30–40 minutes.
2 Leave to cool. Strain through a sieve, and keep in a covered container in the refrigerator. Use within four days. Alternatively, freeze in small amounts and use as required.

VARIATION

For a dark, more richly flavored stock, add a handful of mushroom trimmings or some chopped whole mushrooms.

FRESH TOMATO SOUP

This is the easiest and most delicious tomato soup I know. It is best made in the summer when fresh tomatoes are abundant and deliciously ripe. Use fresh tomatoes; canned tomatoes won't do. Fresh Tomato Soup is also excellent chilled; made with olive oil instead of butter. Serves 4.

INGREDIENTS

*2 tbsps butter **or** 2 tbsps olive oil*
(see note above)
1 medium-sized onion, chopped
4lb fresh tomatoes, quartered
salt and freshly ground black pepper
pinch of sugar
⅔ cup light cream, optional
a few basil leaves, optional

PREPARATION

1 Melt the butter or warm the oil in a large pan over moderate heat, add the onion, cover, and cook until the onion begins to soften: 5 minutes.
2 Add the tomatoes to the pan, cover, and continue to cook until the tomatoes have collapsed and are purée-like: 10–15 minutes.
3 Pour the soup into a food processor or blender and purée, then strain it through a sieve into a clean pan (to serve warm) or into a bowl (to serve chilled), adding a little water to thin it to the desired consistency if necessary. Season with salt and black pepper to taste, and stir in the sugar.
4 Reheat gently, or serve chilled from the refrigerator. If you like, swirl some cream into each bowl and sprinkle a few basil leaves on top.

MUSHROOM, CHEESE, & PARSLEY SOUP

This is a quick soup to make. Although I think it is best puréed, it is also good left just as it is, in which case the cheese should be served separately for everyone to help themselves. A good vegetable stock enhances this soup, but it can also be made with just water, especially if the cheese is strong. Serves 4.

INGREDIENTS

1 tbsp butter
1 tbsp olive oil
1 medium-sized onion, chopped
1 large or 2 medium-sized cloves garlic, chopped
1lb mushrooms, sliced
2½ cups vegetable stock or water
⅔ cup light cream
4 tbsps finely chopped fresh flat-leaf parsley
salt and freshly ground black pepper
¾ cup grated Cheddar cheese

PREPARATION

1 Melt the butter with the oil in a large saucepan over moderate heat, add the onion, cover, and cook until the onion begins to soften: 5 minutes.
2 Add the garlic and mushrooms to the pan, and cook, uncovered, until the mushrooms are tender: 5–10 minutes.
3 Pour in the stock or water, bring to a boil, cover, and cook gently until the vegetables are very tender: about 10 minutes. Remove from the heat, and stir in the cream and parsley.
4 If you prefer not to purée the soup, season it now with salt and black pepper, and serve it immediately, passing the cheese separately.
5 To purée the soup, add the cheese, pour the soup into a food processor or blender, and work until the mushrooms are finely chopped. Taste, and season with salt and black pepper. Return to the pan, reheat gently, without boiling, and serve.

SPINACH SOUP WITH TOASTED PINENUTS

Tender spinach leaves make a delicious green soup, just right for spring and summer. A topping of toasted pinenuts adds an interesting texture and flavor; you can also use toasted flaked almonds if desired. For a slightly sharper flavor, replace a few of the spinach leaves with the same quantity of sorrel. Serves 4.

INGREDIENTS

1 tbsp butter
1 tbsp olive oil
1 medium-sized onion, chopped
3½ cups tender spinach leaves
2½ cups vegetable stock or water
⅔ cup light cream
freshly grated nutmeg
salt and freshly ground black pepper
½ cup pinenuts

PREPARATION

1 Melt the butter with the oil in a large saucepan over moderate heat, add the onion, cover, and cook until the onion begins to soften: 5 minutes. Add the spinach, cover, and cook until it has wilted: about 5 minutes.
2 Pour in the stock or water, bring to a boil, cover, and cook gently until the spinach and onion are very tender: about 15 minutes. Remove from the heat, and stir in the cream.
3 Pour the soup into a food processor or blender and purée it. Add a little water to thin it to the desired consistency, then season well with nutmeg, salt, and black pepper. Return the soup to the pan, and reheat gently without boiling.
4 While the soup is reheating, toast the pinenuts under the broiler until golden brown: about 1–2 minutes.
5 Ladle the soup into bowls and sprinkle toasted pinenuts over each serving.

CLASSIC MINESTRONE

Served with grated cheese on top and plenty of good bread, this soup makes a complete main course. It is also delicious reheated and eaten the following day. Serves 4.

INGREDIENTS

¼ cup olive oil
1 large onion, chopped
3 sticks celery, finely diced
3 large carrots, finely diced
14oz can whole peeled tomatoes in juice
3 cloves garlic, chopped
3 tbsps tomato purée
3 large potatoes, peeled and diced
1 cup medium-sized pasta, such as
macaroni or farfalle
salt and freshly ground black pepper
small bunch of fresh flat-leaf parsley, chopped

PREPARATION

1 Warm the oil in a large saucepan over moderate heat, add the onion, celery, and carrots; cover, and cook for 10 minutes.
2 Pour in the tomatoes, breaking them up with a wooden spoon, then add the garlic, tomato purée, and just under 9 cups of water. Bring to a boil, cover, reduce heat, and cook gently for 10 minutes.
3 Add the potatoes, return to a boil, then cook gently for 10 minutes longer.
4 Drop in the pasta, and cook until the pasta and potatoes are tender: about 10 more minutes. Season with salt and black pepper to taste, and stir in the parsley just before serving.

VARIATIONS

Cabbage is good added to the soup, as are leeks, celeriac, zucchini, and green beans. Canned white beans, such as cannellini, or chickpeas, make filling additions: use the liquid in the can to dilute the soup if necessary.

BEET & APPLE SOUP WITH HORSERADISH CREAM

Using cooked, skinned beets saves time, but make sure you buy beets which have been prepared without vinegar. This soup, a variation on the classic borscht, is lovely for late summer or early autumn. Serve it hot or chilled, depending on the weather. Serves 4.

INGREDIENTS

1 tbsp butter
1 tbsp olive oil
1 medium-sized onion, chopped
2 apples, peeled, cored, and sliced
1 large potato, peeled and diced
¾lb cooked beets, diced
tiny pinch of ground cloves
salt and freshly ground black pepper
squeeze of lemon juice
⅔ cup sour cream
1 – 2 tsps horseradish

PREPARATION

1 Melt the butter with the oil in a large saucepan over moderate heat, add the onion, cover, and cook until tender: 5 minutes. Add the apple and potato, stir well, and reduce the heat. Cover and cook for 10 – 15 minutes longer.
2 Add the beets together with about 4¼ cups of water. Bring to a boil, cover, and cook gently until the vegetables are very tender: about 15 minutes.
3 Pour the soup into a food processor or blender and purée. Add a little more water to thin the soup to the desired consistency, season with ground cloves, salt, and black pepper, and use a squeeze or two of lemon juice to lift the flavor.
4 To serve warm, return to the pan and reheat gently without boiling. To serve cold, transfer to a bowl, allow to cool, and chill in the refrigerator.
5 Pour the cream into a small bowl, and stir in enough horseradish to give it a good tang. Serve the soup in individual bowls with the horseradish cream swirled on top.

VARIATIONS

CHILLED BEET SOUP WITH ORANGE
Make the soup as described, and chill. Stir in the grated zest and juice of half an orange, check the seasoning and serve, without the horseradish.
BEET & CABBAGE SOUP This is more like a traditional borscht. Replace the apple with ½lb thinly sliced cabbage, and don't purée the soup, instead serve it chunky. Sour cream goes well with it, and the horseradish is optional.

GAZPACHO

This Spanish summer soup needs no cooking. Serves 4.

INGREDIENTS

1 red onion
1 green pepper, cored, and seeded
½ large cucumber
1 lb tomatoes, peeled and quartered
4 slices stale white bread
2 cloves garlic
2 tbsps red wine vinegar
2 tbsps olive oil
salt and freshly ground black pepper
1 large ripe plum tomato
croutons (page 47), optional

PREPARATION

1 Cut the onion, pepper, and cucumber into large chunks. Put into a food processor or blender and chop briefly, keeping the texture chunky.

2 Transfer a quarter of the chopped vegetables to a bowl to serve separately later. Cover the bowl, and keep it in the refrigerator.

3 Add the tomatoes, bread, garlic, vinegar, and olive oil to the remainder of the vegetables in the food processor. Blend once more, briefly.

4 If necessary, add enough cold water to the soup mixture to lighten it without making it too thin. Season with salt and black pepper. Transfer to a large serving bowl, cover, and place in the refrigerator to chill.

 You can prepare ahead up to this point. The soup keeps for up to 24 hours in the refrigerator.

5 Finely chop the plum tomato, and add it to the bowl of reserved vegetables.

6 Check and adjust the seasoning of the soup as refrigeration dulls its flavor. Ladle the soup into a chilled bowl, and serve at once. Pass the bowl of reserved vegetables separately, and also, if desired, a bowl of croutons.

CUCUMBER & TARRAGON SOUP

Delicate in flavor, warm or chilled, this soup serves 4.

INGREDIENTS

1 cucumber, peeled and cut into chunks
1 medium-sized onion, chopped
1 clove garlic, peeled
8 – 10 sprigs of fresh tarragon, half of them chopped
4½ cups vegetable stock or water
1 tbsp cornstarch
⅔ cup light cream
2 tbsps lemon juice
freshly grated nutmeg, salt, freshly ground black pepper

PREPARATION

1 Put the cucumber, onion, garlic, unchopped tarragon, and stock or water into a saucepan. Bring to a boil and simmer until the cucumber is tender: about 15 minutes. Allow to cool slightly.
2 Purée in a food processor or blender. Return to the pan, and bring back to a boil.
3 In a small bowl, mix the cornstarch to a smooth paste with a little of the cream, then stir in the rest of the cream. Pour into the soup and stir over moderate heat until the soup has thickened slightly: 2 – 3 minutes.
4 Add the chopped tarragon, lemon juice, nutmeg, salt, and black pepper. Serve at once, warm, or transfer to a bowl to serve later, chilled.

POTATO & LEEK SOUP

Sieving this soup after puréeing it gives it an extra-smooth texture. Try it warm or chilled. When chilled, it is usually called vichyssoise. Serves 4.

INGREDIENTS

1 tbsp olive oil
1 medium-sized onion, chopped
1 lb potatoes, peeled and diced
1 lb trimmed leeks, sliced
4½ cups vegetable stock or water
⅔ cup light cream
freshly grated nutmeg, salt, freshly ground black pepper
chopped fresh chives, to taste

PREPARATION

1 Warm the oil in a large saucepan over moderate heat, add the onion, cover, and cook for 5 minutes. Add the potatoes and leeks, stir well, cover again, and cook for 5 – 10 minutes longer.
2 Pour in the stock or water, bring to a boil, and simmer until the vegetables are tender: about 15 minutes. Allow to cool slightly.
3 Purée in a food processor or blender, then pass through a sieve back into the pan (to serve warm) or into a bowl (to serve chilled).
4 Stir in the cream, and season with nutmeg, salt, and black pepper. Reheat gently, or serve chilled from the refrigerator, with chives on top.

WATERCRESS SOUP

This is delicious warm or chilled. Serves 4.

INGREDIENTS

1 tbsp olive oil
1 medium-sized onion, chopped
1 lb potatoes, peeled and diced
4½ cups vegetable stock or water
1 small bunch watercress, trimmed and roughly chopped
⅔ cup light cream
freshly grated nutmeg, salt, freshly ground black pepper

PREPARATION

1 Warm the oil in a large saucepan over moderate heat, add the onion, cover, and cook for 5 minutes. Add the potatoes, stir well, cover again, and cook for 5 – 10 minutes longer.
2 Pour in the stock or water, bring to a boil, then cover and cook gently until the potatoes are tender: about 15 minutes. Remove from the heat and stir in the watercress.
3 Purée in a food processor or blender. If serving warm, return to the pan. To serve chilled, transfer to a bowl and refrigerate.
4 Stir in the cream, and season with nutmeg, salt, and black pepper. Reheat gently, or serve chilled from the refrigerator.

VARIATION

JERUSALEM ARTICHOKE SOUP Replace the potatoes with the same quantity of Jerusalem artichokes, which should be peeled, diced, and then lightly tossed in lemon juice to prevent discoloration. Omit the watercress. Serve warm or chilled from the refrigerator.

ACCOMPANIMENTS FOR SOUPS

CROUTONS

Sprinkled on soups and salads, croutons add extra flavor and texture. Use slices of stale bread, with the crusts discarded and the bread cut into cubes. Fry the cubes in generous amounts of melted butter and olive oil until golden and crisp all over. Serve them at once, or make them ahead of time and warm them in the oven before serving.

MELBA TOAST

These crisp triangles of thin toast are most easily made from ready-sliced bread. Broil several slices as you would to make ordinary toast, then cut through each slice horizontally to make two thin slices, toasted on one side. Cut into four triangles. Return to the hot broiler, uncooked side up, and toast until golden brown and slightly curled up.

BRUSCHETTA

This is the Italian country version of garlic bread, and it is perfect with minestrone. You need slices of coarse-textured Italian bread, a fat clove of garlic cut in half, and olive oil. Simply slice the bread, toast on both sides, rub with the cut clove of garlic, brush with olive oil, and serve.

GARLIC OR HERB BREAD

For a typically sized French loaf, you need about 6 tbsps butter. For garlic bread, use 2 to 4 fat cloves of garlic, according to taste. Chop the garlic finely, and mash it into the butter.

For herb bread, finely chop fresh herbs, such as parsley, chives, oregano, and marjoram, and mash about 2 tablespoons of them into the butter.

Preheat the oven to 400°F/200°C. Cut into the French loaf at 1-inch intervals without going right through to the base, and press the garlic or herb butter into each crevice.

Wrap in foil, in two parcels if the bread fits the oven better that way, and bake until fragrant and hot inside and crisp outside: about 20 minutes.

CROSTINI

Small crunchy rounds of French bread with savory spreads make a piquant accompaniment to soups. Crostini are particularly good with Olive and Almond Spread or Sundried Tomato Spread (right), or topped with morsels such as cheese, or mushrooms cooked in butter and garlic.

Preheat the oven to 325°F/160°C. Take a thin French baguette and cut it into slices about ½-inch thick. Place on a baking sheet, and dry out in the oven: 10–15 minutes. Brush the slices on both sides with olive oil, and return to the oven to crisp. Allow to cool before adding any topping.

OLIVE & ALMOND SPREAD

Rich and concentrated, a little of this spread goes a long way. Mix all the ingredients together into a smooth paste, softening with a little water if necessary, and serve, spread on crostini, as a snack to go with soup.

INGREDIENTS

⅓ cup black olive purée or well-mashed olives
¾ cup ground almonds
¼ cup finely chopped capers
salt and freshly ground black pepper

VARIATION

SUNDRIED TOMATO SPREAD Replace the black olives with the same quantity of sundried tomatoes in oil, puréed or well mashed. Omit the capers, and add some roughly chopped basil.

SALADS

A salad can be a refreshing accompaniment to a main dish or the distinctive centerpiece of a meal. Composed of cooked or raw ingredients, it can be served warm as well as at room temperature. Probably the most versatile dish in the kitchen, it provides endless possibilities for different combinations of color, flavor, and texture. With such a diversity of salad leaves, oils, and vinegars available, you can enjoy trying out new recipes or experimenting with your own ideas. Leaves are often a key ingredient: store them in the refrigerator where they will keep for several days, then wash and spin, shake, or blot dry on paper towels just before use.

ENDIVE, WATERCRESS, FENNEL, RED ONION, & ORANGE SALAD

This combination of ingredients is particularly refreshing in both color and flavor. The salad does not contain vinegar because the juice of the oranges mingles with the oil to make a light dressing. Serves 4.

Orange

Black pepper

Salt

Olive oil

Garlic

INGREDIENTS

1 clove garlic, peeled and halved
3 tbsps olive oil
salt and freshly ground black pepper
2 – 3 oranges, zest and pith removed, cut on a plate into round slices
2 heads of endive, broken apart
1 bunch watercress, tough stems removed
1 fennel bulb, feathery leaves reserved, thinly sliced
1 red onion, sliced into thin rings

PREPARATION

1 Rub the garlic halves around the salad bowl, and then discard them. Or, for a stronger garlic flavor, crush the garlic and place it in the bowl.
2 Put the oil and a good seasoning of salt and pepper into the bowl. Mix lightly with a fork.
3 Add the orange slices, along with the juice that has collected in the plate.
4 Put the endive and watercress (torn a little if you wish) into the bowl on top of the oranges and dressing. Finally, add the fennel, along with its feathery leaves, and the onion.
5 Toss the salad gently. Serve at once.

Watercress

Fennel

Red onion

Endive

OAK LEAF LETTUCE, AVOCADO, & ROASTED CASHEWS

It is important to assemble this salad just before you serve it so the leaves and cashews remain crisp and the avocado keeps its color. Serves 4 as a first course or accompaniment, 2 as a main course.

INGREDIENTS

1 head of oak leaf lettuce (feuille de chêne)
1 clove garlic, peeled and halved
1 tbsp red wine vinegar
3 tbsps olive oil
salt and freshly ground black pepper
1 ripe avocado
2 tbsps lemon juice
2 tbsps chopped fresh chives
¾ cup cashews, roasted under a hot broiler

PREPARATION

1 Wash and spin or blot dry the oak leaf lettuce.
2 Rub the garlic halves around the salad bowl and then discard them. Or, for a stronger garlic flavor, crush the garlic and place it in the bowl.
3 Put the vinegar, oil, and a good seasoning of salt and pepper into the bowl. Mix lightly with a fork.
4 Halve the avocado, remove the peel and the pit, and slice the flesh. Place in a bowl, sprinkle with the lemon juice, and season with a little salt and black pepper.
5 Tear the salad leaves and scatter them on top of the dressing in the bowl. Add the chives, avocado, and cashews. Toss the salad so that the leaves are lightly coated with dressing and serve at once.

NEW POTATO SALAD

Although new potatoes are best for this, you can use any waxy potatoes that won't break up. Serves 4.

INGREDIENTS

1½lb new potatoes or waxy potatoes, scrubbed
1 tbsp wine vinegar
3 tbsps olive oil
salt and freshly ground black pepper
2 tbsps mayonnaise (for homemade see page 122)
2 tbsps plain yogurt or sour cream
2 tbsps chopped fresh chives

PREPARATION

1 Boil the potatoes until they are just tender, then drain. Either leave the skins on – delicious on new potatoes – or pull them off the potatoes when cool. Cut large potatoes into pieces.
2 Put the vinegar, oil, and a good seasoning of salt and pepper into a bowl. Mix lightly with a fork. Add the potatoes, and turn them over gently in the dressing. Leave to cool completely.

You can prepare ahead up to this point. The salad keeps up to 24 hours in a covered container in the refrigerator.

3 Add the mayonnaise, yogurt or sour cream, and half of the chives to the bowl and mix gently. Taste, and adjust the seasoning if necessary.
4 Transfer to a serving bowl, scatter the remaining chives on top, and serve.

WHITE CABBAGE SALAD

Cabbage salad, or coleslaw, can be served immediately or kept in a covered container in the refrigerator for 24 hours. The flavor improves with keeping. Serves 4.

INGREDIENTS

4 cups white cabbage, shredded
2 carrots, grated
1 shallot or small mild onion, finely chopped
2 tbsps mayonnaise (for homemade see page 122)
2 tbsps plain yogurt or sour cream
2 tbsps chopped fresh chives or other fresh herbs
salt and freshly ground black pepper

PREPARATION

1 Mix the vegetables together in a large bowl.
2 Add the mayonnaise, yogurt or sour cream, herbs, and a good seasoning of salt and pepper. Combine well. Serve at once or keep for later.

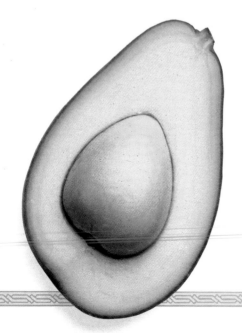

INSALATA TRICOLORE

Taking its name from the Italian flag, this three-colored salad is particularly good as an accompaniment for pasta. Serves 4.

INGREDIENTS

*6 ripe plum tomatoes
2 ripe avocados
1 cup mozzarella cheese, sliced
salt and freshly ground black pepper
several sprigs of fresh basil
1 tbsp red wine vinegar
3 tbsps olive oil*

PREPARATION

1 Cut the tomatoes either across into rounds or downward into long thin slices, cutting out any hard pieces of core.
2 Halve the avocados, remove the peel and the pits, and slice the flesh.
3 On individual plates, arrange alternating slices of tomato, avocado, and mozzarella cheese. Season with salt and black pepper, then tear the basil leaves and sprinkle them over the top.
4 Mix together the vinegar and the oil, and spoon over the salads. Serve at once.

RED & YELLOW CHERRY TOMATOES WITH ORANGE & THYME

This pretty salad makes a change from the more usual tomato and basil salads. It is best made at least half an hour before you want to eat it. Keep it in a cool place but not in the refrigerator, where its flavor would become dulled. Serves 4.

INGREDIENTS

*2 cups red cherry tomatoes, halved
2 cups yellow cherry tomatoes, halved
⅓ cup small black olives, such as niçoise olives
1 tbsp chopped fresh thyme
1 tbsp olive oil
juice and finely grated zest of 1 small orange
salt and freshly ground black pepper*

PREPARATION

1 Put all the ingredients into a bowl and mix them lightly together.
2 Leave to stand for at least 30 minutes in a cool place (not the refrigerator), then mix again. Check the seasoning and serve.

PLUM TOMATOES WITH BASIL

Make this a little ahead of time if you can so that the juices run and the flavors mingle. Keep it in a cool place but not in the refrigerator; serve at room temperature for the flavors to be at their best. Serves 4.

INGREDIENTS

*6 ripe plum tomatoes
1 tbsp red wine vinegar
3 tbsps olive oil
salt and freshly ground black pepper
several sprigs of fresh basil*

PREPARATION

1 Cut the tomatoes either across into rounds or downward into long thin slices, cutting out any hard pieces of core. Place in a shallow dish.
2 Sprinkle with vinegar, oil, salt, and black pepper. Tear the basil leaves and scatter them over the top. Mix the ingredients lightly together.
3 Serve at once or keep in a cool place for later. If serving later, mix again, and check the seasoning.

ROASTED PEPPERS WITH BASIL

This richly flavored salad benefits from being made several hours in advance. Serves 4.

INGREDIENTS

*4 large red and yellow peppers, quartered
2 tsps balsamic vinegar
1 tbsp olive oil
salt and freshly ground black pepper
several sprigs of fresh basil*

PREPARATION

1 Roast and peel the peppers as shown on page 144. Remove the stalk and seeds, and cut the flesh into strips. Place the strips in a shallow dish.
2 Sprinkle with vinegar, oil, salt, and black pepper. Tear the basil leaves and scatter them over the top. Mix the ingredients lightly together.
3 Serve at once, or keep in a cool place for later. If served later, mix again, and check the seasoning.

MIXED LEAF SALAD WITH FLOWERS & HERBS

Without doubt, this is my most useful salad; indeed, it is probably my most versatile vegetable accompaniment. It is quick, healthy, and seems to go with every sort of main course. For variety, add mustard or garlic, flakes of Parmesan, cubes of Gruyère, toasted nuts, or croutons. Illustrated on pages 54–5. Serves 4.

INGREDIENTS

½lb mixed salad leaves, such as oak leaf (feuille de chêne), lollo rosso, frisée, lamb's lettuce, radicchio
1 small bunch arugula or other strongly flavored leaves such as nasturtium or dandelion leaves
2 tsps balsamic vinegar
1 tsp red wine vinegar
3 tbsps olive oil
salt and freshly ground black pepper
1 tbsp chopped fresh tarragon
1 tbsp chopped fresh chives
1 tbsp chopped fresh flat-leaf parsley
¼lb nasturtium flowers or other edible flowers

PREPARATION

1 Wash and spin or blot dry all the salad leaves.
2 Put the vinegars, oil, and a good seasoning of salt and black pepper into a large bowl – you can use the one that you are planning to serve the salad from – and mix lightly with a fork.
3 Cross the salad servers in the base of the bowl, then put in the salad leaves, the herbs, and the flowers. Leave the salad like this, with the crossed salad servers lifting the delicate leaves, herbs, and flowers out of the dressing until just before you want to eat the salad.
4 Toss the salad with the servers, so that all the leaves are lightly coated with dressing, then serve and eat at once.

GREEN LEAVES WITH GOAT CHEESE & WALNUTS

This leafy green salad has toasted goat cheese added to it at the last minute. Make sure the walnuts are fresh and have no trace of bitterness. Serves 4.

INGREDIENTS

*2 lettuces of different types, such as oak leaf (feuille de chêne) and frisée, **or** ½lb mixed salad leaves*
1 clove garlic, peeled and halved
1 tbsp red wine vinegar
2 tbsps olive oil
1 tbsp walnut oil
salt and freshly ground black pepper
¾ cup fresh walnut halves or pieces
1 cup firm goat cheese (the type usually sold in a log), thinly sliced

PREPARATION

1 Wash and spin or blot dry the salad leaves.
2 Rub the garlic halves around the salad bowl and then discard them. Or, for a stronger garlic flavor, crush the garlic and place it in the bowl.
3 Put the vinegar, oils, and a good seasoning of salt and pepper into the bowl. Mix lightly with a fork, and set aside.
4 Toast the walnuts pieces on a baking sheet under a hot broiler until they are lightly browned: 2–3 minutes. Set them aside; leave the broiler on the same setting.
5 Toast the goat cheese on one side on a baking sheet until it is flecked with brown and beginning to melt: 1–2 minutes.
6 Tear the salad leaves and place in the bowl on top of the dressing, add the walnuts, and toss lightly. Distribute the salad among individual plates and put the melting cheese on top. Serve and eat at once.

ARUGULA SALAD WITH FLAKES OF PARMESAN

This delicious, full-bodied mixture of flavors goes particularly well with pasta dishes. Serves 4.

INGREDIENTS

½lb arugula
1 clove garlic, peeled and halved
1 tbsp red wine vinegar
3 tbsps olive oil
salt and freshly ground black pepper
1 cup Parmesan cheese, cut into flakes

PREPARATION

1 Wash and spin or blot dry the arugula.
2 Rub the garlic halves around the salad bowl and then discard them. Or, for a stronger garlic flavor, crush the garlic, and place it in the bowl.
3 Put the vinegar, oil, and a good seasoning of salt and pepper into the bowl. Mix lightly with a fork.
4 Add the arugula, toss it gently in the dressing, scatter the Parmesan over the top, and serve.

VEGETARIAN SALADE NIÇOISE

With crusty bread, this salad makes a filling meal for 4.
Illustrated on page 54.

INGREDIENTS

1½ cups green beans, trimmed
6 ripe plum tomatoes
1 tbsp wine vinegar
4 tbsps olive oil
salt and freshly ground black pepper
14oz can artichoke hearts,
drained and quartered
4 eggs, hardboiled and cut into wedges
4 tbsps chopped fresh flat-leaf parsley
⅔ cup black olives

PREPARATION

1 Place the green beans in a small pan, cover with boiling water, and cook until just tender: 2–4 minutes. Drain and refresh under cold water.
2 Cut the tomatoes either across into rounds or downward into long thin slices, cutting out any hard pieces of core.
3 Put the vinegar, oil, and a good seasoning of salt and pepper into a bowl. Mix lightly with a fork.
4 Add the beans, tomatoes, and remaining ingredients to the bowl, stir gently, and serve.

BEAN & HERB SALAD

Served with bread, this makes a satisfying, light main course, and it can also be served as part of a buffet. A leafy green salad is a good accompaniment. Serves 4.

INGREDIENTS

2 cups fresh shelled or frozen broad beans
1½ cups green beans, trimmed
1 clove garlic, crushed
2 tbsps wine vinegar
6 tbsps olive oil
salt and freshly ground black pepper
14oz can cannellini or navy beans, drained
14oz can chickpeas, drained
3 tbsps chopped fresh herbs, such as
flat-leaf parsley, chives, mint

PREPARATION

1 Place the broad beans in a small pan, cover with boiling water and cook until just tender: 4–5 minutes. Drain. When cool enough to handle, pop them out of their skins with finger and thumb.
2 Place the green beans in a small pan, cover with boiling water, and cook until just tender: 2–4 minutes. Drain, and refresh under cold water.
3 Put the garlic in a bowl with the vinegar, oil, and a good seasoning of salt and black pepper. Mix lightly with a fork to make the dressing.
4 Add the three kinds of beans, the chickpeas, and the herbs. Toss gently to coat them well.

You can prepare ahead to this point. The salad keeps for up to 48 hours in a covered container in the refrigerator.

5 Allow the salad to rest at room temperature for at least an hour, stirring from time to time, so that the flavors develop, then serve.

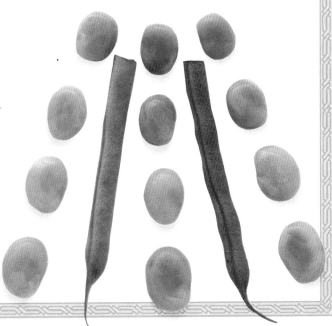

Vegetarian salade niçoise (page 53)

Tabbouleh (page 57)

Mixed leaf salad with flowers and herbs (page 52)

WARM PASTA SALAD WITH TOMATOES & BASIL

A quick and filling pasta dish for 4. It gains richness of flavor from avocado or mozzarella cheese; you could even use both.

INGREDIENTS

*6 ripe plum tomatoes
1lb fusilli or other small chunky pasta
3 tbsps olive oil
salt and freshly ground black pepper
1 cup mozzarella cheese, sliced, **or** flesh of 2 ripe avocados, sprinkled with lemon juice
several sprigs of fresh basil
Parmesan cheese, cut into flakes, optional*

PREPARATION

1 Pour 4 quarts of water into a large pan for the pasta and place over high heat.
2 Cut the tomatoes either across into rounds or downward into long thin slices, cutting out any hard pieces of core.
3 When the water reaches a rolling boil, drop in the pasta. Bring back to a boil, give the pasta a quick stir, then let the water boil steadily until the pasta is *al dente*: tender but not soft right through. Bite a piece to check.
4 Drain the pasta, but leave some water clinging to it, and put it back into the hot pan with the olive oil and a good seasoning of salt and pepper, tossing the pasta so that it is coated with the oil.
5 Add the tomato and the mozzarella or avocado, or both, to the pasta. Tear the basil and stir it in. Check the seasoning and serve at once, strewn with flakes of Parmesan if desired.

WARM PASTA SALAD WITH ROASTED PEPPERS & ARUGULA

This simple dish is colorful, and full of the Mediterranean flavors of rich, sweet peppers and peppery arugula. Serves 4.

INGREDIENTS

*4 large red and yellow peppers, quartered
1lb penne or other small chunky pasta
2 tbsps olive oil
salt and freshly ground black pepper
1 bunch arugula
Parmesan cheese, cut into flakes, optional*

PREPARATION

1 Pour 2½ quarts of water into a large pan for the pasta, and place over high heat.
2 Roast and peel the peppers as shown on page 144. Remove the stalk and the seeds, and cut the flesh into long strips.
3 When the water reaches a rolling boil, drop in the pasta. Bring back to a boil, give the pasta a quick stir, then let the water boil steadily until the pasta is *al dente*: tender but not soft right through. Bite a piece to check.
4 Drain the pasta, but leave some water clinging to it, and put it back into the hot pan with the olive oil, multicolored pepper strips, and a good seasoning of salt and black pepper. Toss the pasta thoroughly so that it is coated with the oil and the pepper strips are warmed through.
5 Tear the arugula roughly and add it to the pasta. Toss gently to distribute the arugula well. Check the seasoning, and serve at once, strewn with flakes of Parmesan if desired.

TABBOULEH

Allow this refreshing dish to stand so that the grains — I prefer couscous to bulgur — soften and absorb the flavors. Illustrated on page 55. Serves 4.

INGREDIENTS

*1½ cups dry, unsoaked couscous or bulgur wheat
4 large tomatoes, roughly chopped
1 green pepper, cored, seeded, and roughly chopped
½ cucumber, roughly chopped
1 clove garlic, crushed
1 red onion, finely chopped
juice of 2 lemons
¼ cup olive oil
6 tbsps chopped fresh flat-leaf parsley
2–3 tbsps chopped fresh mint
salt and freshly ground black pepper*

PREPARATION

1 Put the couscous or bulgur wheat into a bowl.
2 Add all the ingredients, season with salt and pepper, cover, and refrigerate for 12–48 hours. Check and adjust seasoning before serving.

RICE SALAD WITH HERBS, AVOCADO, & NUTS

This salad makes an attractive, fragrant main dish for 4.

INGREDIENTS

*1 cup long grain brown or white rice
½ tsp turmeric powder
sea salt
juice and finely grated zest of ½ lemon
6 tbsps chopped mixed fresh herbs, such as
flat-leaf parsley, mint, chives, and tarragon
1 large ripe avocado
⅓ cup shelled pistachios
⅓ cup cashews, toasted briefly under a hot broiler
salt and freshly ground black pepper*

PREPARATION

1 Cook the rice as described on page 152, adding the turmeric and salt.
2 Add the lemon zest (reserve the juice for later) and herbs, and stir the rice with a wooden fork, mixing them in gently. Leave until the rice is cold.
3 When you are almost ready to eat the salad, halve the avocado, remove the peel and pit, and chop the flesh. Toss the avocado in the reserved lemon juice, then add it to the salad, along with the nuts. Check the seasoning, and serve at once.

WHEAT GRAINS WITH APRICOTS & PINENUTS

This has a Middle Eastern flavor, but it is my own invention. It tastes best if kept in a cool place for several hours before being eaten. Serves 4.

INGREDIENTS

*1 cup wheat grains, brown rice, or millet
2 tbsps olive oil
2 red onions, sliced
1 cup dried apricots, chopped
1 cup raisins
2 tbsps balsamic vinegar
2 tbsps chopped fresh flat-leaf parsley
2 tbsps chopped fresh mint
salt and freshly ground black pepper
1 cup pinenuts, toasted briefly under a hot broiler*

PREPARATION

1 If using wheat grains, cover with cold water and soak for 8 hours or overnight, then boil, covered, for 1¼ hours until tender, adding more water as necessary. If using rice or millet, cook by the absorption method, as described on page 152, allowing only 15–20 minutes for the millet. Drain as necessary, and transfer to a serving bowl.
2 Warm the oil in a large saucepan over moderate heat. Add the onion, cover, and cook gently until tender but still slightly crunchy: about 5 minutes. Remove from the heat, and add the onions and their oil to the grains.
3 Add the apricots, raisins, balsamic vinegar, parsley, and mint, and mix well. Season to taste with salt and black pepper.
4 Stir in the toasted pinenuts, or scatter over the top of the salad just before serving so that they retain their crispness. Serve at once.

VEGETABLE DIPS

Crudités, or pieces of raw vegetables, prepared simply, can be served with dips as part of a buffet, a snack with drinks, or an appetizer. Almost any vegetables may be used: sticks of cucumber, zucchini, celery and carrot, strips of pepper, snow peas, baby corn cobs, radishes, cherry tomatoes, button mushrooms, and so on. In addition to these recipes, try mayonnaise with herbs or garlic (page 122).

GOAT CHEESE DIP

Crudités are ideal for this dip; melba toast or garlicky bruschetta (page 47) are options too. Serves 2 to 4.

INGREDIENTS

½ cup low-fat cream cheese
½ cup firm goat cheese (the type usually sold in a log)
salt and freshly ground black pepper

PREPARATION

1 Put the cream cheese into a bowl, add the goat cheese with its rind, and mash well until the consistency is smooth.
2 Season with salt and black pepper, and spoon into a serving bowl.

VARIATION

BLUE CHEESE DIP Use ½ cup of blue cheese instead of the goat cheese: mash it into the cream cheese as described above.

CUCUMBER & MINT DIP

This refreshing dip is perfect with crudités. Serves 2 to 4.

INGREDIENTS

½ cucumber, peeled and diced
salt
1¼ cups plain yogurt
1 – 2 tbsps chopped fresh mint
½ tsp wine vinegar
freshly ground black pepper

PREPARATION

1 Put the cucumber into a sieve, sprinkle with salt, and leave for at least 30 minutes. This draws out some of the liquid so the dip is not watery.
2 Spoon the plain yogurt into a bowl. Pat the cucumber dry with paper towels, and mix with the yogurt. Add the mint, vinegar, and black pepper to taste. Stir gently, and serve at once.

VARIATION

HERB DIP Replace the cucumber and mint with 4 tablespoons of chopped fresh herbs: tarragon, dill, fennel, basil, oregano, marjoram, cilantro, chives, parsley, and chervil are all possibilities. Instead of vinegar, use lemon juice.

GUACAMOLE

An authentic guacamole contains only avocado, fresh cilantro, tomatoes, and fresh chilis, seasoned with salt and black pepper — add anything else and it becomes an avocado dip. I sometimes serve it on a bed of salad leaves or with red bean dishes. Use really ripe avocados for the best result. Serves 4 to 6.

INGREDIENTS

2 – 3 fresh green chilis, seeded, and finely chopped
4 tomatoes, finely chopped
3 tbsps chopped fresh cilantro
2 large ripe avocados
salt and freshly ground black pepper

PREPARATION

1 Place the chilis, tomatoes, and cilantro in a small bowl.

 You can prepare ahead up to this point. Cover and keep in a cool place until just before you are ready to serve.

2 At the last minute, halve the avocados and remove the pits. Scoop out the flesh and place it in the bowl with the chilis, tomatoes, and cilantro. Use a fork to mash the ingredients together well. Season to taste with salt and black pepper, and serve at once.

CURRIED CASHEW DIP

Crunchy and spicy, this dip goes well with sticks of celery and cucumber. Serves 2 to 4.

INGREDIENTS

1 tbsp olive oil
1 small onion, chopped
1 clove garlic, chopped
2 tsps curry powder
⅔ cup low-fat cream cheese
¼ cup cashews, toasted briefly under a hot broiler
salt and freshly ground black pepper

PREPARATION

1 Warm the oil in a saucepan over moderate heat, add the onion and garlic, cover and cook for 5 minutes. Stir in the curry powder and cook for a further 2 – 3 minutes. Remove from the heat.
2 Put the cheese, onion mixture, and cashews into a food processor or blender and chop finely, then transfer to a serving bowl. Alternatively, put the cheese and onion in a bowl, finely chop the nuts, and stir them in. Season, and serve at once.

HUMMUS

Although hummus is quite widely available, it is so easy to make that if you have a food processor or blender you might as well try the tastier homemade version. Use a light tahini (sesame seed paste); the dark one is too bitter. Serves 2 to 4.

INGREDIENTS

14oz can chickpeas, drained, liquid reserved
1 – 2 cloves garlic
1 tbsp light tahini (see note above)
2 tbsps lemon juice
1 tbsp olive oil
pinch of chili powder, optional
salt and freshly ground black pepper
1 – 2 tbsps cumin seeds, optional

PREPARATION

1 Put the chickpeas, garlic, tahini, lemon juice, and olive oil into a food processor or blender and purée until smooth. Pour in enough of the reserved chickpea liquid to make the consistency like that of lightly whipped cream – you will probably need most, if not all, of the liquid.
2 Add a pinch or two of chili powder to give the hummus a bit of a kick, if desired, then season with salt and black pepper. Transfer to a bowl.
3 Fry the cumin seeds, if using, in a dry pan over moderate heat until they smell aromatic and begin to pop: about 1 – 2 minutes. Sprinkle over the hummus, and serve.

MUSHROOM DIP

Try this with melba toast (page 47). Serves 2 to 4.

INGREDIENTS

1 tbsp butter
1 tbsp olive oil
3 cups button mushrooms, very finely chopped
1 small clove garlic, chopped
½ cup cottage cheese or farmer's cheese
1 tbsp chopped fresh flat-leaf parsley
salt and freshly ground black pepper

PREPARATION

1 Melt the butter with the oil in a large saucepan over moderate heat, and add the mushrooms and garlic. Cook until the mushrooms are tender and just browned: 5 minutes. Remove from the heat.
2 Beat the cottage cheese in a bowl to soften it, then stir in the mushroom and garlic mixture and the parsley. Season, and serve at once.

VEGETABLE DISHES

A hallmark of the new classic vegetarian cookery is exciting and colorful vegetable dishes, inspired by the cuisines of many cultures, as well as by the fresh ingredients themselves. Some dishes, served with bread and a salad, are a satisfying meal on their own. Alternatively, put several together, giving as much variety as possible, for a feast.

Coriander seeds

Garlic

Onion

Fennel

Olive oil

VEGETABLES A LA GRECQUE

"Greek-style," or à la grecque, refers to vegetables cooked in olive oil with a little water and some spices. They are often served cold and so can be made ahead for eating outdoors, for example. The dish is best when fresh new vegetables are plentiful.
Serves 4 as a first course, 2 as a main course.

INGREDIENTS

2 tbsps olive oil
2 medium or 3 small fennel bulbs, thinly sliced,
with feathery leaves reserved
1 medium-sized onion, chopped
2 cloves garlic, crushed
1 tbsp coriander seeds, lightly crushed
4 medium-sized tomatoes, peeled and chopped
½ medium-sized cauliflower, divided into florets
¾ cup green beans, trimmed
1½ cups button mushrooms, halved or quartered
salt and freshly ground black pepper
2–3 tbsps chopped fresh flat-leaf parsley

PREPARATION

1 Warm the oil in a large saucepan over moderate heat, add the fennel (including its feathery leaves) and onion, cover, and cook for 5 minutes. Add the garlic, coriander seeds, and tomatoes and cook, uncovered, until the vegetables are tender and any liquid has disappeared: about 20 minutes.
2 Meanwhile, half-boil, half-steam the cauliflower and green beans: place in a pan, pour in boiling water to ½-inch deep, cover, and cook until just tender: 3–4 minutes. Drain immediately, refresh under cold running water, and leave to dry.
3 Once the fennel and tomato mixture is ready, add the mushrooms and cook gently for a further 3–4 minutes. Stir in the cauliflower and green beans, and season with salt and black pepper. Remove from the heat and set aside.
4 Serve warm or cooled, sprinkled with parsley.

Cauliflower

Green beans

Mushrooms

Salt

Black pepper

Flat-leaf parsley

Tomatoes

MUSHROOM STROGANOFF

*Use a variety of mushrooms: some wild ones,
perhaps, or a mixture of oyster, chestnut, and shiitake
mushrooms, with button mushrooms to make up the
weight. It will seem like a lot of mushrooms, but they
cook down. Serve with boiled rice; for 4.*

INGREDIENTS

*2 tbsps butter
1 tbsp olive oil
2 large onions, chopped
2 cloves garlic, chopped
2lb mushrooms (see introductory note), sliced
1 cup crème fraîche
1 tsp tomato paste
freshly grated nutmeg
salt and freshly ground black pepper
paprika, to garnish*

PREPARATION

1 Melt the butter with the oil in a large saucepan
over moderate heat Add the onion, cover, and
cook for 5 minutes. Add the garlic, and cook for
another 2–3 minutes.
2 Add the mushrooms and cook, uncovered, over
moderate heat until the mushrooms are tender
and much reduced, and most of the liquid has
evaporated: 20–30 minutes.
3 Stir the crème fraîche and tomato paste into the
mixture, turn up the heat, and bring to a boil.
Allow to bubble for 1–2 minutes. Season with
nutmeg, salt, and black pepper and serve,
sprinkled with paprika.

VEGETABLE BOURGUIGNON

Served with baked potatoes, this is a warming meal for 4.

INGREDIENTS

*2 tbsps butter
1 tbsp olive oil
1½ cups pearl onions **or** 1 large onion, sliced
4 cloves garlic, chopped
6–8 medium carrots, sliced
4 large sticks of celery, sliced
4 medium leeks, sliced
3 cups button mushrooms
2 bay leaves
2 tbsps all-purpose flour
2½ cups red wine
1 quart vegetable stock (page 42) or water
salt and freshly ground black pepper
chopped fresh flat-leaf parsley, to garnish*

ROASTED PEPPER RATATOUILLE

*Colorful and delicious, this is one of my standbys.
You can eat it hot with new potatoes, rice, pasta, or
garlic bread, or cold as part of a salad meal. Serves 4.*

INGREDIENTS

*2 red and 2 yellow peppers, quartered
3 tbsps olive oil
2 large onions, chopped
4 cloves garlic, chopped
2 green peppers, cored, seeded, and sliced into rounds
1lb zucchini, sliced
2 x 14oz cans whole peeled tomatoes,
coarsely chopped, with juice
salt and freshly ground black pepper
chopped fresh flat-leaf parsley, to garnish*

PREPARATION

1 Roast and peel the red and yellow peppers as
shown on page 144. Remove the stalk and seeds,
and cut the flesh into strips. Set aside.
2 Heat the oil in a large pan over moderate
heat, add the onion, cover, and cook for 5 minutes.
3 Add the garlic, green peppers, and zucchini and
stir well. Cook, stirring from time to time, for a
further 5 minutes.
4 Pour in the tomatoes. Reduce the heat and let
the mixture simmer, uncovered, until the
vegetables are tender and much of the tomato
liquid has evaporated: 20–30 minutes. Toward
the end of the cooking time, stir in the red and
yellow peppers and allow them to heat through.
5 Season and serve, sprinkled with parsley.

PREPARATION

1 Melt the butter with the oil in a large,
heavy-bottomed pan or casserole dish over
moderate heat. Add the onion, cover, and cook
for 5 minutes.
2 Add the garlic, carrots, celery, leeks,
mushrooms, and bay leaves and stir well. Cover
and cook for a further 5 minutes.
3 Sprinkle the flour over the vegetables. Stir over
the heat with a wooden spoon for 1–2 minutes to
cook the flour.
4 Pour in the wine and stock or water, raise the
heat, and bring to a boil. Reduce the heat,
partially cover the pan, and leave to simmer gently
until the vegetables are tender and the liquid has
reduced: about 1¼ hours.
5 Season to taste with salt and black pepper, and
serve, sprinkled with parsley.

CHILI LIME AVOCADOS

It is important not to overcook these stuffed avocados. They should be left in the oven only long enough to heat through. Illustrated on page 24. Serves 4.

INGREDIENTS

2 tbsps olive oil
1 large onion, chopped
2 cloves garlic, chopped
1–2 fresh green chilis, seeded, and finely chopped
2 large ripe avocados
juice of 1 lime
2 tbsps chopped fresh chives
salt and freshly ground black pepper
thin slices of lime, to garnish

PREPARATION

1 Preheat the oven to 400°F/200°C.
2 Warm the oil in a saucepan over moderate heat, add the onion, and sauté until lightly browned: about 7 minutes.
3 Add the garlic and chilis, stir well, and cook for 5 minutes. Remove from the heat.
4 Halve the avocados, remove the pits, and scoop out the flesh, taking care to leave the skins intact. Chop the flesh into rough chunks and add to the pan of onion and garlic, along with the lime juice, chives, and a good seasoning of salt and black pepper. Mix all the ingredients together well.
5 Place the avocado halves in a greased ovenproof dish, and pile the mixture into them. Bake until heated through: 10 minutes or so. Garnish with thin slices of lime and serve at once.

ZUCCHINI STUFFED WITH ALMONDS & RED PEPPERS

You can serve these in a pool of yogurt and herb sauce or on a bed of Spiced Rice (page 115), with a salad. Illustrated on page 25. Serves 4.

INGREDIENTS

4 medium zucchini, halved lengthwise
2 tbsps olive oil
1 onion, chopped
2 red peppers, cored, seeded, and chopped
2 large cloves garlic, chopped
2 tsps finely chopped fresh thyme
6 tbsps flaked almonds, toasted briefly under a hot broiler
salt and freshly ground black pepper

PREPARATION

1 Preheat the oven to 350°F/180°C.
2 Place the zucchini in a large saucepan, cover with boiling water, and cook until just tender: 3–4 minutes. Drain and allow to cool.
3 Scoop out the seeds with a teaspoon, taking care to leave the skins intact. Chop the seeds and reserve to use in the stuffing. Place the zucchini halves in a greased ovenproof dish.
4 Warm the oil in a saucepan over moderate heat and add the onion and pepper. Cover and cook until they are soft: about 10 minutes. Add the garlic and cook for a further 2 minutes.
5 Remove from the heat and stir in the reserved zucchini seeds, along with the thyme and almonds. Season with salt and black pepper.
6 Spoon the filling into the zucchini halves. Bake until heated through, about 15 minutes, and serve.

*Baby eggplants stuffed
with mushrooms and
pinenuts (below), and herby
stuffed tomatoes (facing page)*

BABY EGGPLANTS STUFFED WITH MUSHROOMS & NUTS

*These baby eggplants, illustrated above, serve 4,
with three halves per person.*

INGREDIENTS

6 baby eggplants, halved lengthwise, stalks left on
1 tbsp olive oil
1 medium-sized onion, chopped
1 clove garlic, chopped
1½ cups button mushrooms, chopped
2 tomatoes, chopped
1 tbsp chopped fresh flat-leaf parsley
¼ cup pinenuts
salt and freshly ground black pepper

PREPARATION

1 Preheat the oven to 350°F/180°C.
2 Place the eggplant halves in a saucepan, cover
with boiling water, and cook until just tender:
3–4 minutes. Drain, and allow to cool.
3 Scoop out the flesh with a teaspoon, leaving the
shells intact. Chop the flesh and reserve. Place the
shells in a greased ovenproof dish.
4 Warm the oil in a pan over moderate heat, add
the onion, cover, and cook for 5 minutes. Stir in
the eggplant flesh, garlic, and mushrooms and
cook for 5 more minutes. Take off the heat, add
the tomato, parsley, and most of the pinenuts
reserving some for decoration, and season well.
5 Spoon the filling into the eggplants, sprinkle
with pinenuts, bake for 15 minutes, and serve.

HERBY STUFFED TOMATOES

Illustrated opposite. Serves 4.

INGREDIENTS

1 shallot or small onion, finely chopped
3 tbsps chopped fresh flat-leaf parsley
1 tsp chopped fresh thyme
¾ cup dried bread crumbs
2 tbsps olive oil
4 beefsteak tomatoes
salt and freshly ground black pepper

PREPARATION

1 Preheat the oven to 350°F/180°C.
(Alternatively, use a preheated broiler).
2 In a bowl, mix together the onion, parsley,
thyme, bread crumbs, and olive oil (if you have a
food processor, put the unchopped onion, parsley,
and thyme into it, along with the bread crumbs
and olive oil, and chop finely to combine).
3 Slice the tops off the tomatoes and reserve
them. Scoop out the seeds with a small teaspoon
to make a cavity for stuffing. You will not need the
inner flesh of the tomatoes for this recipe but you
can chop it and add it to a salad, soup, or sauce.
4 Season the inside of the tomatoes with salt and
black pepper. Spoon in the stuffing, stand the
tomatoes in a greased ovenproof dish, and replace
the tops. Cook in the oven or under a hot broiler
for about 15 minutes, or until heated through but
not collapsing. Serve warm or cold.

CREAM CHEESE MUSHROOMS

Illustrated on page 25. Serves 4.

INGREDIENTS

8 flat mushrooms
⅔ cup cream cheese with garlic and herbs

PREPARATION

1 Preheat the broiler to high.
2 Cut the stems of the mushrooms level with the
gills. Chop up the stems and put into a bowl with
the cream cheese and 2 tablespoons of hot water.
Mix well, then spread over the mushroom gills.
Place the mushrooms in a broiler pan.
3 Grill the mushrooms until the tops are bubbling
and lightly browned and the mushrooms are
tender when pierced with a knife: about 10
minutes. Serve at once.

PEPPERS FILLED WITH ROASTED VEGETABLES

Illustrated on page 24. Serves 4.

INGREDIENTS

2 red and 2 yellow peppers
2 eggplants, cut into ½-inch cubes
1 large onion, sliced
olive oil, for brushing the vegetables
4 tomatoes, quartered
8 fresh basil leaves, lightly torn
1 tbsp balsamic vinegar
salt and freshly ground black pepper

PREPARATION

1 Halve the peppers, cutting down through the
stem, then remove the seeds. Place the peppers,
cut-side down, in a broiler pan, and cook under a
hot broiler for about 10 minutes, until the skins
are charred and blistered. Set aside.
2 Place the eggplants and onion in a broiler pan,
brush with olive oil, and cook under the hot
broiler until tender and lightly browned: about 12
minutes. Turn the vegetables from time to time.
3 Add the tomatoes, turn all the vegetables again,
and cook for another 3–5 minutes.
4 Put the roasted vegetables into a bowl, and
sprinkle the basil, balsamic vinegar, salt, and black
pepper over them. Toss gently.
5 Place the peppers cut-side up in a greased
ovenproof dish, removing or leaving on the papery
skin as you choose. Spoon the roasted vegetable
mixture into the cavities. Serve at once, at room
temperature, or reheat by covering with foil and
placing under a moderate broiler or in a preheated 350°F/180°C oven for about 15 minutes.

PEPPER & BABY CORN COB TERRINE

This delicate terrine has layers of peppers and baby corn cobs separated by thin layers of custard. It requires slow cooking. Serves 6 as a starter, 4 as a main course.

INGREDIENTS

butter and grated Parmesan to coat the pan
3 eggs
3 tbsps light cream
3 tbsps freshly grated Parmesan
salt and freshly ground black pepper
4 large red peppers, roasted and peeled (page 144), and cut lengthwise into wide strips
1 cup baby corn cobs, cooked and drained,
***or** 14oz can baby corn cobs, drained*
1 large yellow pepper, roasted and peeled (page 144), and cut lengthwise into wide strips
sprigs of fresh basil, to garnish

PREPARATION

1 Preheat the oven to 300°F/150°C. Line a 3 x 5 x 9-inch loaf pan with a strip of waxed paper to cover the base and narrow sides. Grease lightly with butter and dust with grated Parmesan.

2 Whisk together the eggs, cream, 2 tablespoons of the Parmesan, and the seasoning. Put 3 tablespoons of this mixture into the prepared pan.

3 Put one thin layer of red pepper into the pan and spoon a little egg mixture over it. Cover with another thin layer of red pepper, a little more egg, a third thin layer of pepper, and a little more egg.

4 Make a layer of whole baby corn cobs, laid lengthwise, and spoon a little egg over it.

5 Make a thin layer of yellow pepper, followed by a little egg, another thin layer of yellow pepper, and a little more egg.

6 Repeat step 4, and then repeat step 3. Pour any remaining egg mixture over the top, and sprinkle with the remaining Parmesan.

7 Bake the terrine in a bain-marie (see page 147) until it is firm to the touch, and a skewer inserted into the center comes out clean: at least 1¼ hours. Allow the terrine to cool thoroughly before removing from the pan.

8 Loosen the terrine by slipping a knife down its two unlined sides. Invert the pan over a plate. Peel off the waxed paper and slice the terrine carefully using a sharp serrated knife in a sawing motion. Serve with thin pesto sauce (page 123) and a garnish of basil.

TERRINE OF VEGETABLES IN A SPINACH COAT

Serves 6 as a starter, 4 as a main course.
Illustrated on page 12.

INGREDIENTS

butter and grated Parmesan to coat the pan
2 cups large fresh spinach leaves, stems removed
6 stalks of asparagus, trimmed to the length of the pan
¾ cup cottage cheese or farmer's cheese
⅔ cup freshly grated Parmesan cheese
2 tbsps chopped fresh chives
2 eggs
salt and freshly ground black pepper
¼ cup sundried tomatoes, sliced
¼ cup artichoke hearts, preserved in oil or canned and drained, sliced

PREPARATION

1 Preheat the oven to 325°F/160°C. Line a 3 x 5 x 9-inch loaf pan with a strip of waxed paper to cover the base and narrow sides. Grease lightly with butter, and dust with grated Parmesan.
2 Bring a saucepan of water to a boil. Drop in the spinach leaves and cook until tender: about 7 minutes. Drain well. Line the pan with the leaves so that they come up the sides and overhang the edges, keeping one or two spare leaves for the top.
3 Place the asparagus in a frying pan, cover with boiling water and cook until tender: 4 – 5 minutes. Drain, and set aside.
4 Put the cottage cheese into a bowl with the Parmesan and chives. Beat in the eggs until the mixture has a smooth, creamy consistency, then season with salt and black pepper. Pour a little of the mixture into the base of the pan.
5 Build up the layers in the pan: asparagus spears laid lengthwise, more cottage cheese mixture, sundried tomatoes, more cottage cheese, artichoke hearts, and the remainder of the cottage cheese. Finally, fold the overhanging spinach over the top, and use the spare leaves to cover the top of the terrine completely.
6 Bake the terrine in a bain-marie (see page 147) until it is firm to the touch and a skewer inserted into the center comes out clean: about 1¼ hours. Allow it to cool thoroughly before turning it out.
7 Loosen the terrine by slipping a knife down its two unlined sides. Invert the pan over a plate to turn out the terrine. Peel off the waxed paper, and slice the terrine carefully using a sharp serrated knife in a sawing motion. Serve on individual plates with sundried tomato sauce (page 120).

GREEN PEA, MINT, & CAULIFLOWER TERRINE

Serves 6 as a starter, 4 as a main course.
Illustrated on page 13.

INGREDIENTS

butter and grated Parmesan to coat the pan
3 cups frozen peas
¾ cup cauliflower florets
3 tbsps butter
3 eggs
salt and freshly ground black pepper
2 tbsps lightly chopped fresh mint, plus a handful of fresh mint leaves

PREPARATION

1 Preheat the oven to 325°F/160°C. Line a 3 x 5 x 9-inch loaf pan with a strip of waxed paper to cover the base and narrow sides. Grease lightly with butter, and dust with grated Parmesan.
2 Place the peas and the cauliflower in separate saucepans, cover with boiling water, and cook until tender: 2 – 3 minutes in each case. Drain.
3 Put the peas into a food processor or blender with 2 tbsps of the butter and 2 of the eggs, and purée. Season with salt and black pepper, and transfer to a bowl.
4 Put half the cauliflower florets into the cleaned food processor or blender with the remaining butter and egg, and purée. Season with salt and black pepper and stir in the chopped mint.
5 Pour just under half of the pea purée into the prepared pan and cover with a good layer of mint leaves. Arrange the whole cauliflower florets on top and pour the puréed cauliflower over them. Cover with the remaining mint leaves in an even layer, and top with the rest of the pea purée.
6 Bake the terrine in a bain-marie (see page 147) until it is firm to the touch and a skewer inserted into the center comes out clean: about 1¼ hours. Allow it to cool thoroughly before turning it out.
7 Loosen the terrine by slipping a knife down its two unlined sides. Invert the pan over a plate to turn out the terrine. Peel off the waxed paper, and slice the terrine carefully using a sharp serrated knife in a sawing motion. Serve on individual plates with a sauce of plain yogurt (stir in a little saffron for color) or with warm homemade hollandaise sauce (page 123).

LENTIL, CARROT, & FENNEL TERRINE

Serves 6 as a starter, 4 as a main course.
Illustrated on page 13.

INGREDIENTS

butter and grated Parmesan to coat the pan
1 small fennel bulb, sliced
2 carrots, sliced
⅓ cup red lentils
1 medium-sized onion, chopped
½ tsp turmeric
⅔ cup light cream
3 eggs
pinch of ground cloves
salt and freshly ground black pepper
small bunch flat-leaf parsley, stalks removed, chopped

PREPARATION

1 Preheat the oven to 325°F/160°C. Line a 3 x 5 x 9-inch loaf pan with a strip of waxed paper to cover the base and narrow sides. Grease lightly with butter, and dust with grated Parmesan.
2 Bring 3 saucepans of water to a boil. Cook the fennel and carrots separately until tender: 10–12 minutes. Drain. In the third saucepan, cook the lentils and onion until tender: about 15 minutes. Drain the lentil and onion mixture, then add the turmeric to boost its color and flavor.
3 Put the lentil and onion mixture into a food processor or blender and purée until smooth. Add the cream and eggs, along with the ground cloves and salt and black pepper to taste, and purée again. Transfer to a bowl.
4 Add the carrot, fennel, and parsley to the lentil purée in the bowl and then, without mixing much, pour the mixture into the prepared pan. Tap the pan briskly several times to make sure the lentil purée runs into all the corners and fills the base completely. Distribute the carrot, fennel, and parsley randomly in the terrine.
5 Bake the terrine in a bain-marie (see page 147) until it is firm to the touch and a skewer inserted into the center comes out clean: about 1¼ hours. Allow it to cool thoroughly before turning it out.
6 Loosen the terrine by slipping a knife down its two unlined sides. Invert the pan over a plate. Peel off the waxed paper and slice the terrine carefully using a sharp serrated knife in a sawing motion. Serve on individual plates with red pepper sauce (page 120).

STRIPED VEGETABLE TERRINE

Serves 6 as a starter, 4 as a main course.
Illustrated on page 12.

INGREDIENTS

butter and grated Parmesan to coat the pan
3 – 4 medium carrots, roughly chopped
1 medium turnip, roughly chopped
2 cups fresh shelled or frozen broad beans
3 tbsps butter
3 tbsps light cream
3 eggs
salt and freshly ground black pepper
6 tbsps finely chopped fresh chervil

PREPARATION

1 Preheat the oven to 325°F/160°C. Line a 3 x 5 x 9-inch loaf pan with a strip of waxed paper to cover the base and narrow sides. Grease lightly with butter, and dust with grated Parmesan.
2 Bring 3 saucepans of water to a boil. Cook the carrots and turnips separately until tender: 10–12 minutes. Drain. In the third saucepan, cook the broad beans until tender: 5 minutes. Drain. When cool, pop off the bean skins using your finger and thumb.
3 Put the carrots into a food processor or blender with a third of the butter, a third of the cream, and 1 egg, and purée until smooth. Season with salt and black pepper. Transfer to a bowl.
4 Repeat the process with the broad beans and the turnips, keeping the purées separate.
5 Pour the carrot purée into the prepared pan and sprinkle with half the chervil in an even layer. Repeat with the broad bean purée, cover with the rest of the chervil, then top with the turnip purée.
6 Bake the terrine in a bain-marie (see page 147) until it is firm to the touch and a skewer inserted into the center comes out clean: about 1¼ hours. Allow it to cool thoroughly before turning it out.
7 Loosen the terrine by slipping a knife down its two unlined sides. Invert the terrine over a plate. Peel off the waxed paper and slice the terrine carefully using a sharp serrated knife in a sawing motion. Serve on individual plates with homemade fresh tomato sauce (page 121).

PUMPKIN, BROCCOLI, & LEEK TERRINE

Serves 6 as a starter, 4 as a main course.
Illustrated on page 12.

INGREDIENTS

butter and grated Parmesan to coat the pan
1¾ cups fresh pumpkin, of which 1 cup is diced and
¾ cup is cut into thin, flat slices
1 cup broccoli florets
4 – 6 thin leeks, the length of the loaf pan
3 tbsps butter
2 cloves garlic, chopped
3 eggs
salt and freshly ground black pepper

PREPARATION

1 Preheat the oven to 325°F/160°C. Line a 3 x 5 x 9-inch loaf pan with a strip of waxed paper to cover the base and narrow sides. Grease lightly with butter, and dust with grated Parmesan.
2 Bring 3 saucepans of water to a boil. Cook the pumpkin, broccoli, and whole leeks separately until tender: test with the point of a knife. Drain.
3 Melt the butter in a small saucepan, add the garlic, and fry for 1 – 2 minutes over moderate heat until the garlic is golden but not browned.
4 Put the garlic with its butter into the food processor or blender, along with the diced pumpkin, eggs, and salt and black pepper to taste. Purée until smooth.
5 Put a thin layer of the purée into the prepared pan, cover with the broccoli florets in an even layer, and cover again with a layer of the purée.
6 Continue to fill up the pan in layers: next use half of the pumpkin slices, then a little more purée, the leeks, enough purée to hold the leeks in place, the remaining pumpkin slices, and finally the remaining purée.
7 Bake the terrine in a bain-marie (see page147) until it is firm to the touch and a skewer inserted into the center comes out clean: about 1¼ hours. Allow it to cool thoroughly before turning it out.
8 Loosen the terrine by slipping a knife down its two unlined sides. Invert the pan over a plate. Peel off the waxed paper and slice the terrine carefully using a sharp serrated knife in a sawing motion. Serve on individual plates with green pepper sauce (page 120) or a little mayonnaise (page 122) mixed into plain yogurt.

BLUE CHEESE, LEEK, & WATERCRESS TERRINE

This is good hot or cold. Served hot it is lovely as part of a Christmas meal, especially accompanied by red wine sauce (page 121). Serves 6 as a starter, 4 as a main course.

INGREDIENTS

butter and grated Parmesan to coat the pan
2 tbsps butter
1 medium-sized onion, chopped
4 medium leeks, sliced
small bunch of watercress, roughly chopped,
with a few sprigs reserved for garnishing
3 eggs, beaten
½ cup blue cheese, crumbled
freshly ground black pepper

PREPARATION

1 Preheat the oven to 325°F/160°C. Line a 3 x 5 x 9-inch loaf pan with a strip of waxed paper to cover the base and narrow sides. Grease lightly with butter, and dust with grated Parmesan.
2 Melt the butter in a medium-large saucepan over moderate heat, add the onion, cover, and cook until tender: about 5 minutes.
3 Add the leeks and watercress to the pan and cook, uncovered, until they are tender and any liquid has evaporated: 5 – 10 minutes. Remove from the heat and allow to cool slightly.
4 Mix the eggs and blue cheese into the cooled mixture. Stir well to combine the ingredients and season with black pepper (no salt because the blue cheese is quite salty). Pour into the prepared pan.
5 Bake the terrine in a bain-marie (see page 147) until it is firm to the touch and a skewer inserted into the center comes out clean: about 1¼ hours. Allow it to cool thoroughly before turning it out.
6 Loosen the terrine by slipping a knife down its two unlined sides. Invert the pan over a plate. Peel off the waxed paper. To serve warm, cover the turned-out terrine in foil and place in a preheated 325°F/160°C oven for about 15 minutes. Slice the terrine carefully using a sharp serrated knife in a sawing motion. Serve warm or cold on individual plates with red wine sauce (page 121).

CASHEW KORMA

Creamy and lightly spiced, this is delicious served with plain boiled rice (page 152). Like many casseroles and spiced dishes, it benefits from being made in advance because the flavors get a chance to develop and blend; it also reheats well. Serves 4.

INGREDIENTS

*3oz creamed coconut, flaked **or** ⅓ cup coconut milk*
2 tbsps sunflower oil
2 medium-sized onions, chopped
2 fresh green chilis, seeded, and finely sliced
2 cloves garlic, chopped
½ tsp ground cumin
½ tsp turmeric
½ tsp ground coriander
1 cup cashews, puréed in a blender or
finely ground in a mouli
salt and freshly ground black pepper
1 cup long grain white or brown rice
½ medium-sized cauliflower, divided into florets
1 cup okra, trimmed
1 cup zucchini, sliced
1 cup frozen peas
2–4 tbsps chopped fresh cilantro

PREPARATION

1 If using creamed coconut, place it in a bowl and cover with 2 cups boiling water. Stir, then leave to melt completely.

2 Warm the oil in a large saucepan over moderate heat. Add the onion, cover, and cook until tender: 5–7 minutes.

3 Add the chilis, garlic, and spices, stir well, and cook for a further 1–2 minutes. Set aside.

4 Add the coconut (the dissolved cream or the milk) and the cashews to the onions and flavorings in the saucepan and season with salt and black pepper. Cover, and set aside once more.

You can prepare ahead to this point. The coconut and cashew mixture keeps for up to 24 hours in a covered container in the refrigerator.

5 Cook the rice as described on page 152.

6 When the rice is almost ready, cook the cauliflower, okra, and zucchini. Pour ½ inch of boiling water into a large saucepan, add the cauliflower and okra, cover, and half-boil, half-steam for 1 minute. Add the zucchini, cover again, and cook for 3 more minutes.

7 Stir the vegetables into the creamy cashew mixture along with the frozen peas. Warm through over gentle heat. Check the seasoning and serve, sprinkled with cilantro, with the rice.

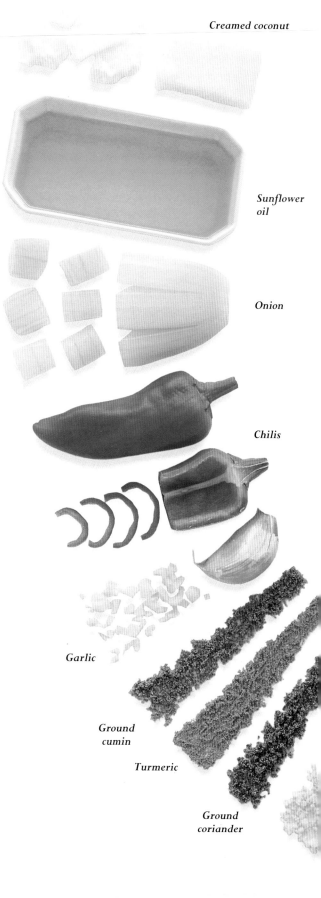

Creamed coconut

Sunflower oil

Onion

Chilis

Garlic

Ground cumin

Turmeric

Ground coriander

Cashews

Salt

Black
pepper

White
rice

Cauliflower

Okra

Zucchini

Peas

Fresh cilantro

CHINESE-STYLE STIR-FRY WITH MARINATED TOFU

Serve this Chinese-style stir-fry with plain boiled rice and provide some extra soy sauce in small bowls; for 4.

INGREDIENTS

MARINATED TOFU

2 cups firm tofu, cut into ½-inch cubes

3 tbsps soy sauce

1 tbsp sesame oil

1 clove garlic, chopped

THE STIR-FRY

2 medium-sized carrots

1 cup bean sprouts

½ cup baby corn cobs

½ cup snow peas

small bunch of scallions

7oz can water chestnuts

7oz can bamboo shoots

½ cup straw mushrooms (from a jar or can)

or 1½ cups button mushrooms

1 tbsp cornstarch

walnut-sized piece of fresh ginger, unpeeled, grated

pinch of five-spice powder

1 tbsp medium sherry

4 tbsps soy sauce

2 tbsps peanut oil

PREPARATION

1 First prepare the tofu, which needs to marinate for around an hour. Put it into a shallow ovenproof bowl that will fit under the broiler. Sprinkle with the soy sauce, sesame oil, and garlic, and stir so that all the tofu is coated. Cover, and set aside.

2 Prepare the vegetables. Slice the carrots very thinly at an angle. Rinse and drain the bean sprouts and baby corn cobs. Trim the snow peas and scallions. Drain the water chestnuts, bamboo shoots, and straw mushrooms. Slice the fresh mushrooms, if using.

3 In a bowl, mix the cornstarch, ginger, five-spice powder, sherry, and soy into a smooth paste.

4 Just before you want to serve the stir-fry, put the marinated tofu under a hot broiler. Turn the pieces of tofu until they are crisp on all sides and heated through: 3–4 minutes.

5 Meanwhile, pour the peanut oil into a wok or a large frying pan and place over high heat.

6 When the oil is smoking hot, put in all the vegetables and stir-fry until evenly heated through but still crisp: about 1–2 minutes.

7 Stir the cornstarch mixture and add it to the wok or pan. Stir-fry for another minute until thickened. Add the tofu, and serve at once.

SUMMER STIR-FRY WITH TOASTED ALMONDS

Summer is the perfect time for a stir-fry: the tender young vegetables and fresh herbs are ideal ingredients. Serves 4.

INGREDIENTS

juice and zest of 1 lemon

1 cup asparagus tips

2 medium-sized zucchini

1 cup baby carrots

1 cup broccoli

1 cup snow peas

1½ cups green beans

2 tbsps peanut oil

4 tbsps chopped fresh flat-leaf parsley

salt and freshly ground black pepper

¾ cup flaked almonds, toasted briefly under a hot broiler

PREPARATION

1 Cut the lemon zest into thin strips. Set the zest and juice aside.

2 Prepare the vegetables. Trim the asparagus tips if necessary. Cut the zucchini into matchsticks. Slice the baby carrots at an angle. Cut the broccoli into florets. Trim the snow peas and green beans.

3 Pour the peanut oil into a wok or a large frying pan, and place over high heat.

4 When the oil is smoking hot, put in all the vegetables, and stir-fry until evenly heated through but still crisp: about 1–2 minutes.

5 Add the lemon zest, 2 tablespoons of lemon juice, the parsley, salt and black pepper, and stir-fry for another minute. Serve at once, with the almonds sprinkled over the top.

VARIATION

To ½ cup of flaked almonds, add ½ cup of pumpkin and sunflower seeds. Spread out in a broiler pan, sprinkle with 4 tbsps of soy sauce, and crisp under a hot broiler: 5–10 minutes, shaking the pan occasionally so they cook evenly. Set aside to cool. Sprinkle over the stir-fry before serving.

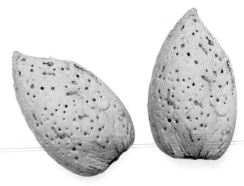

STIR-FRY WITH GOMASIO

Gomasio is a mixture of sesame seeds and salt, toasted and ground to a powder as a piquant topping for stir-fried vegetables. It can be made at home and stored in an airtight container for up to a week. As always, you can vary the vegetables used for the stir-fry, according to your taste and what is available. Serves 4.

INGREDIENTS

THE GOMASIO
6 tbsps sesame seeds
1½ tsps sea salt

THE STIR-FRY
2 bunches of scallions
¾lb daikon (Japanese radish) or turnip
4–6 medium-sized carrots
1½ cups snow peas
2 bunches of radishes
walnut-sized piece of fresh ginger
1 clove garlic
2 tbsps peanut oil
4 tbsps soy sauce

PREPARATION

1 First make the gomasio. Put the sesame seeds and salt into a dry frying pan, and stir over high heat until the seeds smell toasted, turn slightly darker, and start to pop: 1–2 minutes. Remove from the heat and leave to cool, then make into a powder in an electric coffee grinder or a blender. Put into a small bowl for serving.

2 Prepare the vegetables. Trim the scallions or make into tassels as shown on page 145. Cut the daikon or turnip into matchsticks. Dice the carrots. Trim the snow peas. Slice the radishes. Grate the ginger, and chop the garlic.

3 Pour the peanut oil into a wok or a large frying pan, and place over high heat.

4 When the oil is smoking hot, put in all the vegetables, along with the ginger and garlic, and stir-fry until evenly heated through but still crisp: about 1–2 minutes.

5 Add the soy sauce, and stir-fry for another minute. Serve at once, with the gomasio in a small bowl or sprinkled over the stir-fry.

PARMIGIANA DI MELANZANE

Traditionally, this southern Italian eggplant pie is made with fried eggplants. This can make the dish rather oily, so I boil or steam the slices of eggplant instead. With the richness of the cheeses and the oil in the tomato sauce, I find the result just right. Serve with bread, a leafy salad, and some red wine. For 4.

INGREDIENTS

1½lb eggplants, thinly sliced
2 tbsps olive oil
2 medium-sized onions, chopped
2 cloves garlic, chopped
2 x 14oz cans whole peeled tomatoes, coarsely chopped, with juice
salt and freshly ground black pepper
1 cup mozzarella cheese, sliced
⅔ cup freshly grated Parmesan cheese

PREPARATION

1 Preheat the oven to 400°F/200°C.
2 Steam or boil the eggplants until just tender. To steam them, you may need to do them in more than one batch, depending on the size of the steamer, but they take only a few minutes.
3 Meanwhile, warm the oil in a medium-large saucepan over moderate heat, add the onions, cover, and cook for 5 minutes. Add the garlic and cook for another minute.
4 Pour in the tomatoes together with their juice, and cook, uncovered, until the liquid evaporates and the mixture has reduced: about 15 minutes. Season with salt and black pepper. This is the tomato sauce.
5 Put a layer of eggplant slices into a shallow, lightly greased, ovenproof dish. Cover with slices of mozzarella and a little tomato sauce. Repeat the layers until the ingredients have been used, ending with a layer of tomato sauce. Sprinkle the Parmesan cheese over the top.
6 Bake, uncovered, until golden brown and bubbling: 25–30 minutes. Serve at once.

VARIATIONS

This eggplant pie is best made with good mozzarella cheese packed in water. Alternatives would be another Italian cheese, such as Bel Paese, or – totally inauthentic but still delicious – slices of Brie or Camembert. For a complete change, you can make a version of this dish using slices of cooked potato instead of half, or all, of the eggplant. It ceases then to be Parmigiana di Melanzane but is delicious and filling all the same.

ZUCCHINI & TOMATO GRATIN

This is one of my favorite summer dishes. With new potatoes and salad, it makes a light meal. Serves 4 as a first course, 2 as a main course.

INGREDIENTS

2 tbsps butter
3 tbsps olive oil
1½lb zucchini, thinly sliced
1 medium-sized onion, chopped
1 clove garlic, chopped
4 medium fresh tomatoes, peeled and roughly chopped
salt and freshly ground black pepper
½ cup fresh bread crumbs

PREPARATION

1 Preheat the oven to 400°F/200°C.
2 Melt the butter with 1 tablespoon of the oil in a large saucepan over moderate heat, and add the zucchini. Cover and cook until just tender: 5–7 minutes. You may need to cook the zucchini in two batches, depending on the size of the pan.
3 Meanwhile, warm the rest of the oil in a medium-large saucepan over moderate heat. Add the onion, cover, and cook for 5 minutes. Add the garlic, and cook for another minute.
4 Reduce the heat, add the tomatoes to the onions, cover, and cook until they have collapsed and any water they give off has evaporated: about 15 minutes. Season well with salt and black pepper. This is the tomato sauce.
5 Stir the zucchini into the tomato sauce and pour into a shallow, lightly greased, ovenproof dish. Make the top level, sprinkle it with bread crumbs, and dot with the remaining butter.
6 Bake, uncovered, in the oven until the top is golden brown and crisp: 25–30 minutes. Serve hot.

VARIATIONS

LEEK GRATIN is the winter version. Replace the zucchini with the same weight of trimmed leeks. Slice the leeks thinly and cook gently in the butter and oil until tender: about 15 minutes. Add to the tomato sauce and continue as above.
PARSNIP, POTATO, OR KOHLRABI GRATIN Replace the zucchini with the same weight of parsnips, potatoes, or kohlrabi, cut into slices about ¼-inch thick and steamed or boiled until just tender. Arrange the vegetables in the casserole dish in layers, spreading each layer with the tomato sauce.

ROASTED MEDITERRANEAN VEGETABLES

This is one of the easiest vegetable dishes to prepare and one of the most versatile and delicious. The amount of garlic may seem large – a whole bulb rather than just a clove or two – but when roasted it becomes very mild in flavor. It doesn't need peeling before cooking or serving; just pop the cloves of garlic out of their skins at the table and eat the creamy insides. Serves 4, with a substantial plateful each.

INGREDIENTS

3 fennel bulbs
3 red peppers
3 eggplants
3 red onions
olive oil
1 garlic bulb
3 tbsps balsamic vinegar
fresh basil leaves, to taste
salt and freshly ground black pepper

PREPARATION

1 Preheat the oven to 450°F/230°C.
2 Trim the fennel, removing any of the outer layers that seem too tough. Slice through each bulb from top to bottom, cutting it first into halves, then into quarters, then eighths. Each segment will be held together by its share of the root end. Steam or parboil the fennel for about 8 minutes, or until it is just tender without being soggy. Drain and dry well with paper towels.
3 Cut the peppers into chunks, discarding the seeds and core. Don't peel them; it is easy to scoop the tender sweet flesh away from the skin after they are roasted, and some people like to eat the roasted skin.
4 Trim the eggplants and cut them into chunks.
5 Peel the onions and slice them into eighths in the same way as the fennel.
6 Brush all these prepared vegetables with olive oil, put them into a roasting pan, and roast for approximately 20 minutes.
7 Remove the roasting pan from the oven. Break the garlic into cloves and add these, unpeeled, to the pan, turning the other vegetables as necessary to allow them to roast evenly. Return the vegetables to the oven, reduce the heat to 350°F/180°C, and roast until tender and browned in places: about 15 – 20 minutes more.
8 Transfer to a serving dish, sprinkle with the vinegar and some torn basil leaves, and season with salt and black pepper. Serve hot or warm.

ROASTED ROOT VEGETABLES

A mixture of different root vegetables, roasted together, makes a warming winter dish. Vary the vegetables according to what is available, and serve with a nutritious dipping sauce such as hummus (page 59) if desired. The quantities given here serve 4, with a substantial plateful each.

INGREDIENTS

2 medium-sized celeriac
10–12 medium-sized parsnips
10–12 medium-sized carrots
3 large potatoes
6 tbsps olive or peanut oil
crunchy sea salt

PREPARATION

1 Preheat the oven to 450°F/230°C.
2 Once the oven is hot, pour the oil into two roasting pans and place them in the oven to heat up.
3 Prepare the vegetables as necessary, and cut them into even-sized pieces.
4 Put the vegetables into the hot oil, spooning oil over them so that they are coated all over, then roast for 20 minutes.
5 Reduce the heat to 350°F/180°C. Turn the vegetables to allow them to cook evenly, then continue to roast until crisp outside and tender inside: about 15 – 20 minutes more.
6 Remove from the oven, blot on paper towels, sprinkle with sea salt, and serve immediately.

VEGETABLE TEMPURA

This Japanese-inspired dish of vegetables in crisp, light batter makes a delicious treat. Many different vegetables can be used: cut into small pieces for quick cooking, or parboil first, which is the best way to prepare cauliflower and broccoli florets, for example. Serve the tempura the minute they are done, with the dipping sauce on the side. As a main course, serve with plain boiled rice.
Serves 4 as a first course, 2 as a main course.

INGREDIENTS

1 medium-sized carrot, cut into matchsticks
1 red onion, thinly sliced
½ cup snow peas, trimmed
1½ cups shiitake mushrooms, thinly sliced
THE DIPPING SAUCE
walnut-sized piece of fresh ginger, unpeeled, grated
*2 tbsps mirin (sweet rice wine) **or** 1½ tsps clear honey*
dissolved in 1 tbsp hot water
3 tbsps soy sauce
THE BATTER
1 egg
1 cup all-purpose flour, sifted with
a pinch of salt
½ cup tepid water
FOR FRYING
oil such as peanut

PREPARATION

1 Have all the prepared vegetables at hand.
2 Mix together the ingredients for the dipping sauce. Pour into individual bowls.
3 The batter, which does not need to stand, should be made at the last minute. Break the egg into the flour and salt, and mix lightly with a fork. Add the water and stir to make a batter – it should not be completely smooth.
4 Pour about 3 inches of oil into a large saucepan or deep-fat fryer and place over high heat.
5 When the oil reaches a temperature of 350°F/ 180°C – when bubbles form on a wooden chopstick or the handle of a wooden spoon dipped into it – coat three or four pieces of vegetable with the batter and drop them into the oil.
6 Fry the tempura until crisp underneath (about 1 minute), then turn them over with a slotted spoon, and fry the other side for 1 minute. Drain on paper towels, but don't cover them or they will lose their crispness.
7 Quickly skim any scraps from the oil using a slotted spoon and discard. Put in another small batch of freshly battered vegetables. Continue until all the vegetables are fried, and serve at once with the dipping sauce.

Shiitake mushrooms

Snow peas

Red onion

Carrot

Soy sauce

Fresh ginger

Mirin

Batter

Peanut oil

CREPE GATEAU

Crêpes – layered with a rich-tasting eggplant mixture and topped with creamy béchamel sauce and Parmesan cheese, garnished with bright red cherry tomatoes and sprigs of fresh oregano – make a wonderful main course that looks dramatic when brought to the table. Slice it into thick wedges as for a cake. Serves 4 to 6.

INGREDIENTS

THE CREPES
1 quantity of crêpe batter (page 149)
olive oil for frying the crêpes

THE FILLING
¼ cup olive oil
2 large onions, chopped
4 large cloves garlic, chopped
3 medium-sized eggplants, finely diced
½ cup all-purpose flour
2 x 14oz cans whole peeled tomatoes, coarsely chopped, with juice
1½ cups red wine
½lb button mushrooms, sliced
2 tbsps chopped fresh oregano
salt and freshly ground black pepper

THE TOPPING
2 cups freshly made béchamel sauce (page 148)
⅔ cup light cream
freshly grated nutmeg
⅓ – ⅔ cup freshly grated Parmesan cheese
cherry tomatoes and sprigs of oregano, to garnish

PREPARATION

THE CREPES
1 Make the batter as described and place it next to the stove with a ladle.
2 Brush a frying pan measuring about 8 inches across the base (or a slightly larger than standard crêpe pan) with a little olive oil and place over high heat. Once the olive oil is hot enough to sizzle when a drop of water is dropped into it, take the pan off the heat and ladle in enough batter to coat the base. Return to the burner and let the crêpe cook until the top is set and lightly browned: about 1 minute. Flip it over.
3 Cook the second side until lightly browned: just a few seconds. Lift the crêpe out of the pan onto a piece of foil. Reheat the pan – you won't need to regrease it every time – and make five more crêpes in the same way, stacking them up. Cover with foil until you need them.

 The crêpes can be prepared ahead of time. Wrap in foil and keep in the refrigerator for up to 3 days, or in the freezer for up to 3 months.

THE FILLING
1 Warm 3 tbsps of the oil in a large saucepan over moderate heat, add the onions and garlic, cover, and cook for 5 minutes. Then stir in the eggplant, cover, and cook until tender: 15 – 20 minutes. Stir from time to time.
2 Sprinkle the flour onto the eggplant, stir over the heat for another minute or two, then pour in the tomatoes with their juice and the red wine. Continue to stir over the heat until the mixture thickens, then reduce the heat, cover, and leave for 8 – 10 minutes to cook the flour. Remove from the heat.
3 In another pan, warm the remaining tablespoon of oil over moderate heat, add the mushrooms, and fry until tender and lightly browned: 3 – 5 minutes. Drain the mushrooms of any liquid and add them to the eggplant mixture. Stir in the oregano, and season with salt and black pepper.

TO ASSEMBLE AND BAKE
1 Preheat the oven to 400°F / 200°C. Place one of the crêpes (thawed if necessary) on a large ovenproof plate. Cover it evenly with a fifth of the eggplant mixture (it should make a thick layer). Put another crêpe on top, cover with another fifth of the eggplant mixture, and so on, finishing with a crêpe on top.
2 Gently warm the béchamel sauce, then stir in the cream. Check the seasoning, adding some nutmeg. Pour enough sauce over the crêpe gateau to cover the top and run attractively down the sides. The rest can be poured into a pitcher to be served alongside the gateau.
3 Sprinkle the Parmesan on top of the gateau and bake, uncovered, until it is heated right through and golden brown on top: about 20 minutes. Garnish with cherry tomatoes and sprigs of oregano, and serve immediately.

MUSTARD SEED CREPES WITH SPICED VEGETABLE FILLING

Mustard seeds give these crêpes a crunchy texture and a bit of a kick, but they are not hot. The filling, too, is spicy but mild. The recipe has no exotic source; it was just an idea I had one day when I wanted to make a spicy dish with a difference. Mango chutney and a tomato and onion salad go well with the crêpes. Serves 4 to 6.

INGREDIENTS

THE CREPES
1 quantity of crêpe batter (page 149)
2 tbsps mustard seeds
olive oil for frying the crêpes

THE FILLING
2 tbsps olive oil
1 large onion, chopped
2 cloves garlic, chopped
½ tsp turmeric
2 tsps cumin seeds
2 large potatoes, peeled and diced
2 cups fresh young spinach leaves
salt and freshly ground black pepper

PREPARATION

THE CREPES
1 Preheat the oven to 350°F/180°C so that you can keep the crêpes warm as they are done (unless you are preparing them in advance to eat later). Make the batter as described, stir in the mustard seeds, and place the batter next to the stove with a ladle. Stir the batter each time you make a crêpe to keep the seeds well distributed.

2 Brush a crêpe pan (or a small frying pan measuring about 6 inches across the base) with olive oil, and place over high heat. Once the olive oil is hot enough to sizzle when a drop of water is flicked into it, take the pan off the heat and ladle in enough batter to coat the base. Return to the heat, and let the crêpe cook until the top is set and lightly browned: about 1 minute. Flip it over carefully.

3 Cook the second side until lightly browned: just a few seconds. Lift the crêpe out of the pan onto a piece of foil. Reheat the pan – you won't need to regrease it every time – and make the rest of the crêpes in the same way, stacking them up. Cover with foil until you need them.

 The crêpes can be prepared ahead of time. Wrap in foil and keep in the refrigerator for up to 3 days, or in the freezer for up to 3 months.

THE FILLING
1 Warm the oil in a large saucepan over moderate heat, add the onion, and fry for 5 minutes. Stir in the garlic and spices and stir-fry, for 1 – 2 minutes.
2 Stir in the potatoes, coating them well with the oil and spices. Then add the spinach, and cook, stirring, until the spinach and potatoes are tender: about 10 – 12 minutes. Season to taste.

TO ASSEMBLE
1 Preheat the oven to 350°F/180°C.
2 Spread the filling thinly over each crêpe (thawed if necessary), roll them up, and place them side by side in a lightly greased, 9 x 13-inch casserole dish. Cover with aluminum foil, reheat for 20 minutes, and serve at once.

VEGETABLE SIDE DISHES

Creamy potato gratins, vegetable ribbons with pesto, warm and spicy red cabbage, puréed celeriac, buttered leeks: vegetables are flavorful, healthy, and highly adaptable ingredients. Vegetarian meals are often loosely structured, and a range of simple, lightly cooked vegetable side dishes can accompany a more elaborate main dish or even play the starring role in a meal. Whatever your choice, aim for interesting colors and textures in a meal.

GRATIN DAUPHINOIS

This dish adds a touch of luxury to any meal — and it couldn't be easier to make. Serves 4.

INGREDIENTS

3 large potatoes, peeled
3 tbsps butter
1 – 2 cloves garlic, chopped
freshly grated nutmeg, salt, freshly ground black pepper
¾ cup heavy cream
½ pint milk

PREPARATION

1 Preheat the oven to 300°F/150°C.
2 Cut the potatoes into the thinnest slices possible: use a food processor with a slicing disc if you have one. Rinse the potatoes in a bowl of water and place in a colander to drain.
3 Grease a casserole dish with half the butter. Scatter the garlic over the base of the dish, then put in the potatoes in even layers, seasoning with nutmeg, salt, and pepper as you go. Pour in the cream and milk, and dot with the rest of the butter.
4 Bake, uncovered, until the potatoes are tender when pierced with a knife and the top layer is golden and crisp: 1½–2 hours. Serve at once.

WILD MUSHROOM GRATIN DAUPHINOIS

Serves 4.

INGREDIENTS

⅔oz dried wild mushrooms
3 large potatoes, peeled
3 tbsps butter
1 – 2 cloves garlic, chopped
salt and freshly ground black pepper
¾ cup heavy cream
½ pint milk

PREPARATION

1 Preheat the oven to 300°F/150°C.
2 Put the mushrooms in a small bowl, cover with boiling water, and leave to soak for a few minutes. Meanwhile, follow step 2 for Gratin Dauphinois.
3 Drain and chop the reconstituted mushrooms.
4 Grease a casserole dish with half the butter and scatter the garlic into the dish. Make a layer of potatoes, then of mushrooms, season with salt and black pepper, and continue until the ingredients are used up, finishing with potatoes. Pour in the cream and milk, and dot with the rest of the butter.
5 Follow step 4 for Gratin Dauphinois.

TOMATO GRATIN DAUPHINOIS

Serves 4.

INGREDIENTS

3 large potatoes, peeled
4 tbsps olive oil
1 clove garlic, chopped
6 medium-sized tomatoes, peeled and chopped
salt and freshly ground black pepper
fresh basil leaves, roughly torn, to taste

PREPARATION

1 Follow steps 1 and 2 for Gratin Dauphinois.
2 Grease a casserole dish with half the oil, and scatter the garlic into the dish. Make a layer of potato, then of tomato, season with salt and black pepper, and continue until all the ingredients are used up, finishing with a layer of potatoes. Pour the remaining oil on top.
3 Follow step 4 for Gratin Dauphinois. Serve garnished with fresh basil.

FANTAIL ROAST POTATOES

An attractive variation on roast potatoes. You can follow
steps 1 and 2 ahead of time, and put the potatoes in the
hot oven later. To serve 4, use 2 pounds of potatoes
and ¼ cup of melted butter.

1 Peel and halve the potatoes. Cut fine slits in the top of each one, without going through the base, so the potato stays intact.

2 Parboil the potatoes for 5 minutes. Drain. Stand them on a greased baking sheet, and brush all over with melted butter.

3 Preheat the oven to 400°F / 200°C. Bake the potatoes until golden and crisp outside, and tender inside: 40 – 60 minutes. Serve at once.

ROSTI WITH SAGE

*Crisp, fragrant, and delicious, rosti is best made in one
big round, which you cut into wedges to serve. Instead of
sage, try rosemary or thyme, or even 1 to 2 tablespoons
of crushed juniper berries. Serves 4.*

INGREDIENTS

4 large potatoes, skins left on
salt
2 tbsps chopped fresh sage
olive or sunflower oil for frying

PREPARATION

1 Place the potatoes in a saucepan, cover with
cold water, bring to a boil and cook for about 5
minutes. Drain and leave to cool.
2 Slip the skins off the potatoes using a small
sharp knife and your fingers. Grate the potatoes
coarsely, season with salt, and add the herbs.
3 Pour enough oil into a large frying pan to cover
the base, and place over moderate heat. Once the
oil is hot, put in the potatoes, pressing down with
a spatula to make one big round. Fry until crisp
and brown underneath: about 8 minutes. Tip the
rosti out onto a plate, cooked-side up, and then
slide it back into the pan to cook the second side.
4 Continue to cook until the second side is
browned and crisp, then drain on paper towels
and serve at once.

POTATO PANCAKES

*This is a quick, simple, and delicious way to prepare
potatoes. They make a good snack, and children
in particular love to eat them with ketchup
and baked beans. Serves 4.*

INGREDIENTS

2 large potatoes, peeled
1 small onion
1 tbsp all-purpose flour
2 eggs, beaten
salt and freshly ground black pepper
olive or sunflower oil for frying

PREPARATION

1 Grate the raw potatoes coarsely. Rinse
the grated potato at once, then drain, pat dry, and
transfer to a bowl.
2 Grate the onion over the potatoes. Sprinkle
with the flour, pour in the eggs, and season with
salt and black pepper. Stir to combine.
3 Pour enough oil into a frying pan to cover the
bottom, and place over moderate heat. Once the
oil is hot, drop in tablespoonfuls of the potato
mixture, flattening each mound with the back of
the spoon. Fry the pancakes until crisp and brown
underneath: about 3 minutes. Turn them over and
cook the other side. The potato inside will be
tender by the time both sides are crisp.
4 Serve at once, or keep warm in the oven.

TAGLIATELLE OF CABBAGE

Cabbage is cut into long strands to resemble tagliatelle, then tossed in butter and an aromatic spice. This dish is better made with a soft whitish green cabbage than with a very hard white one. Serves 4.

INGREDIENTS

1 medium cabbage
1 tbsp butter
*freshly grated nutmeg, whole caraway seeds, **or** powdered cinnamon*
salt and freshly ground black pepper

PREPARATION

1 Remove and discard the tough central stem of the cabbage, then slice the leaves into long thin strands to resemble tagliatelle. You can use either a knife or a vegetable peeler to do this.
2 Pour ½ inch of boiling water into a saucepan and add the cabbage. Cover the pan, and half-boil, half-steam the cabbage over moderate heat until just tender: 5–7 minutes (most of the cabbage will be out of the water: it steams rather than boils, retaining flavor and nutrients). Drain.
3 Transfer the cabbage to a bowl, and add the butter, along with the spice of your choice, salt and pepper to taste. Toss well, and serve at once.

CARROT & ZUCCHINI RIBBONS WITH PESTO

The vegetables are sliced into long strands and mixed with fragrant pesto for this pretty, summery dish. Illustrated on page 84. Serves 4.

INGREDIENTS

4 large carrots, peeled
2 medium-sized or large zucchini
2 tbsps pesto (for homemade, see page 123)
salt and freshly ground black pepper

PREPARATION

1 Cut the carrots and zucchini into long, fine strands or ribbons by drawing a vegetable peeler down the length of them.
2 Pour ½ inch of boiling water into a saucepan and add the carrots. Cover the pan, and half-boil, half-steam the carrots over moderate heat for 2–3 minutes. Add the zucchini and cook for 1–2 minutes longer (zucchini cook quickly; don't let them become waterlogged). Drain.
3 Transfer the vegetables to a bowl, add the pesto and a little seasoning, mix well, and serve at once.

JULIENNE OF KOHLRABI

Kohlrabi is a root vegetable rather like turnip, with a delicate flavor and a pleasantly crunchy texture. Its smooth skin is pale green or purple. Serves 4.

INGREDIENTS

6 medium kohlrabi
1 tbsp butter
salt and freshly ground black pepper

PREPARATION

1 Peel the kohlrabi thinly; I find a vegetable peeler best for this. Cut the flesh into julienne strips (see page 145).
2 Pour ½ inch of boiling water into a saucepan and add the kohlrabi. Cover the pan, and half-boil, half-steam the kohlrabi over moderate heat until just tender: about 2 minutes. Drain.
3 Transfer the kohlrabi to a bowl, and add the butter, salt, and black pepper to taste. Toss well, and serve at once.

JULIENNE OF BEETS

A quick and delicious way to serve beets. Use ready-cooked beets if you wish, but choose ones that have been prepared without vinegar. Serves 4.

INGREDIENTS

6 medium beets
juice and zest of 1 orange
1 tbsp butter
salt and freshly ground black pepper

PREPARATION

1 Trim off any leaves from the beets, leaving at least 4 inches of stem still attached to prevent the color of the beets from bleeding as they cook. Place in a saucepan, cover with cold water, and bring to a boil. Reduce the heat, cover, and cook until the beets are tender when pierced with the point of a knife: at least 1 hour.
2 Allow to cool, then peel off the skin using your fingers and a sharp knife, and cut the beets into julienne strips (see page 145). Place in a saucepan.

You can prepare the beets several hours ahead to this point.

3 Remove the bitter pith from the orange zest and cut the zest into long thin strips. Add the orange zest and juice to the beets, along with the butter, and season to taste. Cover, heat through, and serve at once.

GREEN BEANS WITH CUMIN

I love green beans and find they go with many dishes. When very young and tender, they can be steam-boiled whole and need no embellishment. When they are bigger, trim them, and jazz them up with some spicy cumin seeds. Serves 4.

INGREDIENTS

4½ cups green beans, trimmed
1 tbsp butter
1 tbsp olive oil
2 tsps cumin seeds
salt and freshly ground black pepper

PREPARATION

1 Pour ½ inch of boiling water into a saucepan and add the green beans. Cover the pan, and half-boil, half-steam the beans over moderate heat until just tender but still crisp: 2–5 minutes depending on size. Drain and transfer to a bowl.
2 Melt the butter with the oil in a frying pan over moderate heat. Add the cumin seeds and stir until they begin to pop and smell aromatic: 1–2 minutes. Pour the seeds along with the butter and oil over the beans. Toss the beans lightly, season to taste, and serve at once.

CELERIAC PURÉE

One of the nicest ways to serve the root vegetable celeriac is as a creamy purée, with plenty of salt and freshly ground black pepper. Sometimes I use celeriac on its own, but I find a mixture of potato and celeriac works particularly well because the potatoes add a starchy creaminess to the mixture. Serves 4.

INGREDIENTS

1 large celeriac
1 large potato
1 tbsp butter
a little milk or light cream
salt and freshly ground black pepper

PREPARATION

1 Peel the celeriac and the potato. I find a sharp knife best for celeriac and a vegetable peeler for potatoes. Cut into even-sized chunks, place in a saucepan, and cover with boiling water. Put the lid on the pan and simmer the vegetables gently until tender: 15–20 minutes.
2 Drain, saving the water for stock. Add the butter, and mash with a potato masher (a food processor makes the potatoes gluelike), adding milk or light cream for a soft consistency. Season with salt and black pepper. Serve at once or keep warm in a bain-marie on the stove for up to 1 hour.

BUTTERED LEEKS WITH PARSLEY

Tender, not-too-large leeks are best for this, but in any case, try to get leeks that are of similar diameter so they cook in the same amount of time. Serves 4.

INGREDIENTS

8 medium leeks
1–2 tbsps butter
2 tbsps finely chopped flat-leaf parsley
freshly grated nutmeg
salt and freshly ground black pepper

PREPARATION

1 Trim the leeks and wash off any dirt as shown on page 147.
2 Pour ½ inch of boiling water into a large saucepan or frying pan and lay the leeks in it. Cover and half-boil, half-steam until tender: 7–10 minutes, depending on size. Drain, and transfer to a bowl that can accommodate them lengthwise.
3 Add the butter, parsley, and freshly grated nutmeg. Season with salt and black pepper, toss the leeks well, and serve at once.

SPINACH WITH NUTMEG

If you can get tender spinach leaves, wilting them in a little olive oil is more successful than boiling them: it retains their bright green color and fresh taste. You need a large saucepan for this; it may be easier to cook in two batches. Serves 4.

INGREDIENTS

6 cups tender young spinach leaves
2 tbsps olive oil
freshly grated nutmeg
salt and freshly ground black pepper

PREPARATION

1 Wash the spinach thoroughly in 2 or 3 changes of cold water, then put it into a colander to drain.
2 Heat a tablespoon of oil in a large saucepan over high heat. Add half the spinach and stir-fry until it has just wilted and warmed through: 1–2 minutes. Remove from the heat and transfer to a warmed bowl. Cook the second batch of spinach in the same way, using the remaining oil.
3 Stir in the nutmeg, salt, and pepper, and serve.

*Carrot and zucchini
ribbons with pesto
(page 82)*

*Bombay potatoes
(page 86)*

Spiced red cabbage and apple (page 87)

SPICED OKRA

*Okra is a vegetable you either love or hate. I love it;
I find that its fresh flavor and glutinous texture
lend themselves especially well to spicy mixtures
such as this. Serves 4.*

INGREDIENTS

*2 tbsps peanut or sunflower oil
1 medium-sized onion, chopped
2 cloves garlic, chopped
2 tsps ground cumin
2 tsps ground coriander
3 cups okra, stalks removed,
cut into ¼-inch lengths
14oz can whole tomatoes, coarsely
chopped, with juice
salt and freshly ground black pepper
2–4 tbsps chopped fresh cilantro, to garnish*

PREPARATION

1 Warm the oil in a medium-sized saucepan
over moderate heat, add the onion, cover, and
cook for 5 minutes.
2 Add the garlic, cumin, and ground coriander
and cook for 2 minutes, stirring from time to time.
3 Add the okra and cook for a further 2 minutes,
stirring from time to time.
4 Pour in the tomatoes with their juice and cook,
uncovered, until the okra is tender and the excess
tomato liquid has evaporated to make a thick
sauce: 15–20 minutes.
5 Season with salt and black pepper to taste, and
serve, sprinkled with chopped cilantro.

BOMBAY POTATOES

*These golden potatoes can be served as a side dish
with a curry or a pilau, or with any bean or grain
dish when you want to add a little spiciness.
Illustrated on page 85. Serves 4.*

INGREDIENTS

*2 tbsps peanut or sunflower oil
1 medium-sized onion, chopped
2 cloves garlic, chopped
2 tsps ground cumin
2 tsps ground coriander
½ tsp turmeric
¼ tsp cayenne pepper
3 large potatoes, peeled and
cut into ½-inch cubes
salt
1 tsp garam masala
freshly ground black pepper
2–4 tbsps chopped fresh cilantro, to garnish*

PREPARATION

1 Warm the oil in a medium-sized saucepan
over moderate heat, add the onion, cover, and
cook for 5 minutes.
2 Add the garlic, cumin, ground coriander,
turmeric, and cayenne and cook for 2 minutes,
stirring from time to time.
3 Add the potatoes, and stir well to coat them
with the onion, garlic, and spices. Add a teaspoon
of salt and pour in ⅔ cup of water, bring to a boil,
then cover and cook over gentle heat until the
potato is just tender and most of the water has
disappeared: about 10–15 minutes.
4 Stir in the garam masala. Taste the mixture. If
you like, add more salt, some black pepper, and, if
you want a hotter dish, some more cayenne. Serve
warm or cool, sprinkled with chopped cilantro.

SPICED RED CABBAGE & APPLE

This aromatic vegetable dish is just as good, if not better, when reheated. It is a warming dish to make as part of a winter meal and is the perfect accompaniment for a baked potato filled with sour cream and chives. Illustrated on page 85. Serves 4.

INGREDIENTS

2 tbsps butter
1 tbsp peanut or sunflower oil
1 large onion, chopped
3 medium apples, peeled, cored, and chopped
1 medium red cabbage, shredded
pinch of ground cloves
½ tsp ground cinnamon
½ cup raisins, optional
1 tbsp brown sugar
1 tbsp red wine vinegar
salt and freshly ground black pepper

PREPARATION

1 Melt the butter with the oil in a large saucepan over moderate heat, add the onion, cover, and cook for 5 minutes.
2 Add the apples, stir, cover, and cook for a further 2 – 3 minutes.
3 Add the cabbage to the pan and pour in 2 cups of water. Stir in the cloves, cinnamon, raisins, sugar, and vinegar. Reduce the heat, cover, and cook until the cabbage is tender: about 1 hour.
4 Season well with salt and black pepper, and serve at once or reheat later.

ROASTED POTATOES WITH GARLIC & ROSEMARY

This is a good way to prepare potatoes toward the end of summer when they are larger. I generally leave the skins on the boiled potatoes, but they slip off easily with a knife. Serves 4.

INGREDIENTS

3–4 large potatoes, scrubbed
olive oil, to brush over the potatoes
4 cloves garlic, peeled
3–4 sprigs of fresh rosemary
sea salt and freshly ground black pepper

PREPARATION

1 Cut the potatoes into even-sized pieces for cooking. Put in a saucepan, cover with water, and boil until they are almost tender when pierced with the point of a knife. Drain and cool. Slip off the skins if desired. Cut the potatoes into slices about ¼-inch thick.
2 Preheat the broiler to high.
3 Place the potatoes in a single layer on an oiled baking sheet or in a broiler pan, and brush with olive oil. Broil until they are crisp and golden brown on one side, then turn over and repeat on the other side.
4 Roughly chop the garlic and rosemary, and sprinkle over the potatoes a few minutes before they are done. If you add them too soon, they will burn and the flavor will be spoiled.
5 Sprinkle with sea salt, grind some black pepper over them and serve at once.

PASTA

Pasta is popular with just about everyone: quick to cook, and the basis for many exciting and delicious meals. A dish of pasta with one of the tempting sauces on these pages creates a complete meal that can be made in minutes. With a little more time, you can put together a wonderful baked pasta dish – spinach, tomato, and mozzarella lasagna, for example – that is perfect for entertaining. Prepare it ahead of time and relax when your guests arrive.

LINGUINE WITH CREAM & HERB SAUCE

Serves 4.

INGREDIENTS

1 tbsp butter
1 shallot or small onion, chopped
1¾ cups crème fraîche
salt and freshly ground black pepper
1lb linguine
1 tbsp olive oil
*2 – 4 tbsps chopped fresh herbs such as parsley,
chives, and chervil*
freshly grated Parmesan cheese, optional

PREPARATION

1 Pour 4½ quarts of water into a large pan for the pasta, and place over high heat.
2 Melt the butter in a medium-sized saucepan over moderate heat, add the shallot or onion, cover, and cook until tender: about 4 minutes.
3 Add the crème fraîche, heat to boiling point, and cook, stirring, until thick and creamy: 2 – 3 minutes. Season with salt and black pepper and keep warm.
4 When the water reaches a rolling boil, drop in the pasta. Bring back to a boil, give the pasta a quick stir, then let the water boil steadily until the pasta is *al dente*: tender but not soft right through. Taste a piece to check.
5 Drain the pasta, but leave some water clinging to it, and return it to the hot pan with the olive oil and a good seasoning of salt and black pepper. Toss the pasta so that it is coated with the oil.
6 Add the sauce to the pasta, together with the fresh herbs. Toss the pasta, making sure that it is well coated with the sauce, and serve at once, with freshly grated Parmesan if desired.

FARFALLE WITH BROCCOLI CREAM SAUCE

Serves 4.

INGREDIENTS

1 tbsp butter
1 shallot or small onion, chopped
1¾ cups crème fraîche
salt and freshly ground black pepper
½ cup broccoli florets
1lb farfalle, or other chunky pasta
1 tbsp olive oil
freshly grated Parmesan cheese, optional

PREPARATION

1 Pour 4½ quarts of water into a large pan for the pasta, and place over high heat.
2 Melt the butter in a medium-sized saucepan over moderate heat, add the shallot or onion, cover, and cook until tender: about 4 minutes.
3 Add the crème fraîche, heat to boiling point and cook, stirring, until thick and creamy: 2 – 3 minutes. Season with salt and black pepper and keep warm.
4 Put the broccoli in a small pan, cover with boiling water, and cook until just tender: 2 – 3 minutes. Drain well, and stir into the sauce.
5 To cook and serve the pasta, follow steps 4 to 6 of Linguine with Cream and Herb Sauce, omitting the fresh herbs in step 6.

TAGLIATELLE WITH MUSHROOM CREAM SAUCE

Serves 4.

INGREDIENTS

1 tbsp butter
1 shallot or small onion, chopped
1½ cups button mushrooms, sliced
1¾ cups crème fraîche
salt and freshly ground black pepper
1lb tagliatelle
1 tbsp olive oil
freshly grated Parmesan cheese, optional

PREPARATION

1 Pour 4½ quarts of water into a large pan for the pasta, and place over high heat.
2 Melt the butter in a medium-sized saucepan over moderate heat, add the shallot or onion, cover, and cook for 2 minutes. Add the mushrooms and cook until tender: around 2 minutes.
3 Add the crème fraîche, heat to boiling point and cook, stirring, until thick and creamy: 2–3 minutes. Season with salt and black pepper, and keep warm.
4 To cook and serve the pasta, follow steps 4 to 6 of Linguine with Cream and Herb Sauce (page 88), omitting the fresh herbs in step 6.

SPAGHETTI WITH BLUE CHEESE SAUCE

Serves 4.

INGREDIENTS

1 tbsp butter
1 shallot or small onion, chopped
1¾ cups crème fraîche
salt and freshly ground black pepper
1lb spaghetti
1 tbsp olive oil
¼–½ cup Dolcelatte or Gorgonzola cheese, crumbled
freshly grated Parmesan cheese, optional

PREPARATION

1 Follow steps 1 to 5 of Linguine with Cream and Herb Sauce (page 88).
2 Add the sauce to the pasta, together with the blue cheese. Toss the pasta, making sure that it is well coated with the sauce, and serve at once, with freshly grated Parmesan, if desired.

SPINACH, TOMATO, & MOZZARELLA LASAGNA

Rich-tasting lasagna in abundance, with plenty of leafy salad and good bread, makes an excellent spread for a party, whatever the age group. Lasagna can be difficult to prepare but it is based on two simple sauces, tomato and béchamel, that can be made ahead of time. Indeed, the whole lasagna can be assembled in advance and kept refrigerated until you want to bake it for ravenous guests. Serves 4.

INGREDIENTS

1 tbsp butter
*2 cups frozen spinach **or** fresh tender spinach leaves*
salt and freshly ground black pepper
½lb lasagna
1 quantity of basic tomato sauce (page 121), prepared ahead
½ cup mozzarella cheese, thinly sliced
⅔ cup light cream
1 quantity of béchamel sauce (page 148)
⅓–⅔ cup freshly grated Parmesan cheese

PREPARATION

1 Preheat the oven to 350°F/180°C, unless preparing the lasagna ahead to bake later.
2 Melt the butter in a large saucepan over moderate heat, add the spinach, and cook until tender: 7 minutes for fresh spinach, 2–3 minutes for frozen. Drain well, press out excess water, and season with salt and black pepper.
3 Parboil the pasta: pour 4½ quarts of water into a large saucepan and bring to a boil. Drop several sheets of the pasta into the boiling water, and cook for a few seconds. Retrieve the sheets with a slotted spoon, drape them over the sides of a colander to prevent them from sticking together, and cook the next batch.
4 Grease a 3 x 9 x 13-inch ovenproof dish or baking pan. Cover the base with sheets of lasagna, and build up the layers as follows: half of the tomato sauce, all of the spinach, another layer of lasagna, the rest of the tomato sauce, all of the mozzarella, the rest of the lasagna.
5 Stir the cream into the béchamel sauce and pour evenly over the lasagna. Sprinkle Parmesan on top.

You can prepare ahead to this point. Keep the assembled lasagna in a cool place or the refrigerator until you are ready to bake it.

6 Bake the lasagna until bubbling and golden brown on top: 40–50 minutes. Serve at once.

SPAGHETTI WITH FRESH TOMATO SAUCE

Though this is one of the simplest pasta sauce recipes, the combination of perfectly cooked pasta and fresh tomato sauce is hard to beat. Once familiar with the basic recipe, you can vary it by adding other ingredients and flavorings of your choice. Two cans of tomatoes in juice can be used instead of the fresh tomatoes: cook uncovered until most of the liquid has evaporated, leaving you with a thick sauce. Serves 4.

INGREDIENTS

*3 tbsps olive oil
1 large onion, chopped
2 cloves garlic, chopped
8 medium tomatoes, peeled and chopped
salt and freshly ground black pepper
1 lb spaghetti
fresh Parmesan cheese, cut into flakes, optional
fresh basil leaves, to garnish*

PREPARATION

1 Pour 4½ quarts of water into a large pan for the pasta and place over high heat.
2 Warm 2 tbsps of the olive oil in a saucepan over moderate heat, add the onion, cover, and cook until tender: about 5 minutes. Add the garlic and cook for a further 2 minutes.
3 Reduce the heat, add the tomatoes, cover, and cook until they have collapsed and the sauce has thickened: 10–15 minutes. Season to taste with salt and black pepper, and keep warm.
4 Meanwhile, when the water reaches a rolling boil, drop in the pasta. Bring back to a boil, give the pasta a quick stir, then let the water boil steadily until the pasta is *al dente*: tender but not soft right through. Taste a piece to check.
5 Drain the pasta but leave some water clinging to it, and return it to the hot pan with the remaining tablespoon of oil and a good seasoning of salt and black pepper. Toss the pasta to coat it with the oil.
6 Add the sauce to the pasta, and toss it well, making sure that the pasta is well coated with the sauce. Serve at once, with flakes of Parmesan if desired, and basil leaves to garnish.

PENNE ARRABBIATA

This is a tomato sauce with chili added to give it a kick. Like the previous recipe, it is very easy to make — the whole dish can be made from start to finish in about 20 minutes. Serves 4.

INGREDIENTS

*3 tbsps olive oil
1 large onion, chopped
2 cloves garlic, chopped
1 fresh green chili, seeded, and finely chopped
2 x 14oz cans whole peeled tomatoes, coarsely chopped,
with juice
salt and freshly ground black pepper
1 lb penne, or other tubular pasta
such as rigatoni
fresh Parmesan cheese, cut into flakes, optional
fresh basil leaves, to garnish*

PREPARATION

1 Pour 4½ quarts of water into a large pan for the pasta, and place over high heat.
2 Warm 2 tbsps of the olive oil in a saucepan over moderate heat, add the onion, cover, and cook until tender: about 5 minutes. Add the garlic and chili and cook for a further 2 minutes.
3 Pour in the tomatoes with their juice and cook, uncovered, until the excess tomato liquid has evaporated and the sauce has reduced: 10–15 minutes. Season to taste with salt and black pepper, and keep warm.
4 Meanwhile, when the water reaches a rolling boil, drop in the pasta. Bring back to a boil, give the pasta a quick stir, then let the water boil steadily until the pasta is *al dente*: tender but not soft right through. Taste a piece to check.
5 Drain the pasta, but leave some water clinging to it, and return it to the hot pan with the remaining tablespoon of olive oil and a generous seasoning of salt and black pepper. Toss the pasta to coat it with the oil.
6 Add the sauce to the pasta, and toss it well, making sure that the pasta is well coated with the sauce. Serve at once, with flakes of Parmesan if desired, and basil leaves to garnish.

RIGATONI WITH TOMATO, EGGPLANT, & RED PEPPERS

This sauce goes well with a tubular pasta, such as rigatoni, or a long pasta, such as spaghetti. It benefits from slower cooking, becoming a rich sauce that is delicious accompanied by a leafy green salad and a glass of red wine. Serves 4.

INGREDIENTS

3 tbsps olive oil
1 large onion, chopped
1 medium-sized eggplant, finely diced
1 red pepper, cored, seeded, and finely diced
1 clove garlic, chopped
2 x 14oz cans whole peeled tomatoes, coarsely chopped, with juice
salt and freshly ground black pepper
1lb rigatoni
fresh Parmesan cheese, cut into flakes, optional
fresh basil leaves, to garnish

PREPARATION

1 Warm 2 tbsps of the olive oil in a saucepan over moderate heat, add the onion, cover, and cook until tender: about 5 minutes. Add the eggplant, pepper, and garlic, cover, and cook for a further 5 minutes, stirring occasionally.
2 Pour in the tomatoes with their juice, reduce the heat, and cook slowly, uncovered, until the excess liquid has evaporated and the sauce is thick and purée-like: 20–25 minutes. Season to taste with salt and black pepper and keep warm.
3 Pour 4 ½ quarts of water into a large pan over high heat and bring to a boil. Drop in the pasta, give it a quick stir, then let the water boil steadily until the pasta is *al dente*: tender but not soft right through. Bite a piece to check.
4 Drain the pasta but leave some water clinging to it, and return it to the hot pan with the remaining olive oil and a good seasoning of salt and black pepper. Toss the pasta to coat it with the oil.
5 Pour in the sauce and toss the pasta once more. Serve at once, with flakes of Parmesan if desired, and basil leaves to garnish.

EGGS & CHEESE

Delicious and versatile foods in their own right, eggs and cheese are invaluable ingredients in many tempting dishes, from the lightest of soufflés to vibrant, savory roulades and simple omelettes. To offset their richness, serve these dishes with fresh fruit and vegetables, cereals, and bread.

CHEESE FONDUE

A delicious, runny cheese fondue is usually a winner. It is too rich to eat every day, but it is perfect for a small party, when spearing cubes of bread onto a fork and dipping them into the fondue is all part of the fun, and so, too, is scraping out the delicious crusty cheese residue in the bottom of the pan. You need a burner to stand the saucepan of cheese on: a fondue pot or a hot plate will do. Serves 4.

INGREDIENTS

1 clove garlic, peeled and halved
1¼ cups dry white wine
2 cups Gruyère cheese, grated
2 cups Swiss cheese, grated
1 tsp potato flour or cornstarch
2 tbsps kirsch
freshly grated nutmeg
salt and freshly ground black pepper
1 large baguette, cut into bite-sized pieces and warmed in the oven, to serve

PREPARATION

1 Rub the garlic around the inside of a medium-sized saucepan, then discard it. Put the wine and cheeses into the saucepan and heat gently, stirring often with a wooden spoon until the cheese has melted and the mixture comes just to a boil. Remove from the heat.
2 Mix the potato flour or cornstarch with the kirsch, and stir into the cheese mixture. Return to the heat, and stir until the fondue thickens and coats the back of the spoon. Season with nutmeg, salt, and black pepper.
3 Place the pan of fondue in the center of the table on a burner, and serve with the warmed bread cubes. Forks are best for spearing the cubes of bread and dipping them into the fondue. The fondue becomes thicker the longer it stands on the burner, and it leaves a lovely cheesy residue in the bottom of the pan which should also be eaten.

SPINACH SOUFFLE

A basic soufflé mixture can be flavored with a variety of different ingredients, and one of the best is spinach. For an even more flavorful soufflé, add the Parmesan cheese. Serves 3 to 4.

INGREDIENTS

¼ cup butter, plus extra to grease the dish
3½ cups frozen chopped spinach or fresh young spinach leaves
6 tbsps all-purpose flour
1¼ cups milk
5 egg whites, 4 egg yolks
½ cup freshly grated Parmesan cheese, optional
freshly grated nutmeg
salt and freshly ground black pepper

PREPARATION

1 Melt 1 tbsp of the butter in a large saucepan over moderate heat, and add the spinach. For frozen spinach, cook until it has thawed and any water has evaporated: 2–3 minutes. For fresh spinach, cook until it wilts: about 7 minutes. Drain, squeezing out excess water, and chop.
2 Melt the rest of the butter, stir in the flour, and slowly add the milk to make a béchamel sauce, as shown on page 148. Leave to cool slightly.
3 Stir the egg yolks into the sauce and mix well. Stir in the spinach and, if desired, the Parmesan. Season with nutmeg, salt, and pepper.

You can prepare ahead up to this point. The spinach mixture and the egg whites keep for several hours, covered, in the refrigerator.

4 Preheat the oven to 400°F/200°C. Butter a 1½-quart soufflé dish and tie a piece of buttered waxed paper around the outside extending at least 2 inches above the rim.
5 To finish making the soufflé and to bake it, follow steps 4–6 on page 26 of Classic Dishes.

TWICE-BAKED GOAT CHEESE & THYME SOUFFLES

The easiest soufflés are these small, twice-baked ones;
bake them once, then put them aside. Later, turn
them out of their molds and place in a baking dish.
Return to a hot oven until golden and puffed up.
Serves 6 as a first course, 3 as a main course.

INGREDIENTS

¼ cup butter
6 tbsps all-purpose flour
1¼ cups milk
5 egg whites, 4 egg yolks
½ cup firm goat cheese (preferably with rind),
cut into ¼-inch dice
salt and freshly ground black pepper
butter and grated Parmesan to coat the custard cups
1¼ cups light cream, optional
¾ cup soft fresh bread crumbs
2 tbsps chopped fresh thyme

PREPARATION

1 Melt the butter, stir in the flour, and slowly add the milk to make a béchamel sauce, as shown on page 148. Leave to cool slightly.
2 Stir the egg yolks into the sauce. Add the goat cheese, and season with salt and black pepper.
3 Preheat the oven to 400°F/200°C. Butter 6 custard cups and sprinkle with grated Parmesan.
4 In a clean bowl, whisk the egg whites until they are stiff. Stir 2 tablespoons of the egg whites into the cheese mixture, then gently fold in the rest using a metal spoon. Pour the mixture into the custard cups.
5 Put the custard cups into a bain-marie (see page 147), and place in the oven. Turn the temperature down to 375°F/190°C. Bake the soufflés until risen and a skewer comes out clean: 15–20 minutes. Remove from the oven and leave to cool in their containers; they will sink a great deal.

You can prepare ahead up to this point. Keep the soufflés in their containers in the refrigerator for 2–3 days or in the freezer for several weeks.

6 Preheat the oven to 425°F/220°C. Remove the soufflés from the custard cups then place in a shallow, ovenproof dish. Pour the cream, if desired, over and around them. Mix together the bread crumbs and thyme, and sprinkle generously over the top. Bake until risen, heated through, and golden brown: about 15 minutes. Serve at once from the baking dish.

TWICE-BAKED MUSHROOM SOUFFLES

Serves 6 as a first course, 3 as a main course.

INGREDIENTS

¼ cup butter
¼lb button mushrooms, chopped
6 tbsps all-purpose flour
1¼ cups milk
5 egg whites, 4 egg yolks
3 tbsps chopped mixed fresh herbs, such as parsley,
marjoram, chives, and thyme
¼ cup Gruyère cheese, grated
salt and freshly ground black pepper
butter and grated Parmesan to coat the custard cups
1¼ cups light cream, optional
⅓ cup freshly grated Parmesan cheese, optional

PREPARATION

1 Melt the butter in a medium-sized saucepan over moderate heat, add the mushrooms, and cook, uncovered, for 2–3 minutes.
2 Stir in the flour and slowly add the milk to make a béchamel sauce, as shown on page 148. Leave to cool slightly.
3 Stir the egg yolks into the sauce. Add the herbs, half the Gruyère, and season with salt and pepper.
4 Preheat the oven to 400°F/200°C. Butter 6 custard cups and sprinkle with grated Parmesan.
5 In a clean bowl, whisk the egg whites until they are stiff. Stir 2 tablespoons of the egg whites into the mushroom mixture, then fold in the rest, using a metal spoon. Pour the mixture into the custard cups.
6 Put the custard cups into a bain-marie (see page 147), and place in the oven. Turn the temperature down to 375°F/190°C. Bake the soufflés until risen and a skewer comes out clean: 15–20 minutes. Remove from the oven, and leave to cool in their containers; they will sink a great deal.

You can prepare ahead up to this point. Keep the soufflés in their containers in the refrigerator for 2–3 days or in the freezer for several weeks.

7 Preheat the oven to 425°F/220°C. Remove the soufflés from the custard cups then place in a shallow, ovenproof dish. Pour the cream, if desired, over and around the soufflés, sprinkle with the rest of the Gruyère and the Parmesan to taste. Bake until risen, heated through, and golden brown: about 15 minutes. Serve at once from the baking dish.

CHEESE ROULADE BASE

*The roulades on the right are made with this cheese base.
They are illustrated on pages 36 – 7. Each serves
6 as a starter, 4 as a main course.*

INGREDIENTS

*butter and grated Parmesan for coating
¼ cup cottage cheese or farmer's cheese
⅔ cup light cream
4 eggs, separated
1 cup Gruyère or Cheddar cheese, grated
3 tbsps chopped fresh herbs, such as thyme, marjoram,
and parsley, optional
salt and freshly ground black pepper
freshly grated Parmesan cheese to garnish, optional*

PREPARATION

1 Preheat the oven to 400°F/200°C. Line a
9 x 13-inch shallow-sided baking sheet with
waxed paper. Grease the paper lightly with butter,
and sprinkle with Parmesan cheese.
2 Put the cottage cheese into a large bowl, add
the cream, and mix until smooth. Beat in the egg
yolks one by one. Finally, stir in the grated cheese,
and the herbs, if desired, and season to taste.
3 In a separate clean bowl, whisk the egg whites
until they are stiff. Fold the egg whites into the
cheese mixture using a metal spoon, then pour the
cheese and egg white mixture into the prepared
pan, smoothing it to the edges. Bake until risen
and just firm in the center: 12 – 15 minutes.
4 Place a piece of waxed paper large enough for
the roulade next to the oven and sprinkle it with
Parmesan. Take the roulade out of the oven and
place it, face down, onto the paper. Remove the
waxed paper that was used to line the pan from
the top of the roulade.
5 Allow the roulade to become cool to the touch
before covering with the chosen filling mixture
and rolling up as shown opposite. Sprinkle the
finished roulade with freshly grated Parmesan, if
desired. It may be served at once or reheated later.
Some roulades, such as Gruyère and Herbs with
Arugula (right), benefit from being cooled in the
refrigerator before serving.

*Roulades may be prepared in advance and
reheated. Wrap in foil and place in a preheated
325°F/160°C oven for 15 minutes.*

Roulade fillings

GRUYERE WITH RED PEPPERS

INGREDIENTS

*4 large red peppers, quartered
½ cup cottage cheese or farmer's cheese
cheese roulade base, using Gruyère and omitting herbs*

PREPARATION

1 Roast and peel the peppers as shown on page
144, removing the core and seeds.
2 Soften the cottage cheese with about 2 tbsps of
water. Spread it over the roulade base, cover with
the peppers, and roll up as shown. Serve with
quick herb sauce (page 123).

CHEDDAR & HERBS WITH MUSHROOMS

INGREDIENTS

*2 tbsps butter
1¼lb mushrooms, thinly sliced
2 cloves garlic, finely chopped
salt and freshly ground black pepper
cheese roulade base, using Cheddar and herbs*

PREPARATION

1 Melt the butter in a saucepan over moderate
heat, add the mushrooms and garlic, and cook
until the mushrooms are tender and the liquid has
evaporated: 12 – 15 minutes. Season to taste.
2 Cover the base with the mushrooms and roll up
as shown. Serve with red wine sauce (page 121).

GRUYERE & HERBS WITH ARUGULA

INGREDIENTS

*cheese roulade base, using Gruyère and herbs
2 ripe avocados
2 tbsps lemon juice
1 small bunch arugula, thinly sliced*

PREPARATION

1 Cover the roulade base with a damp dish cloth
and set aside to cool; this roulade is best eaten cold.
2 Mash the flesh of the avocados with the lemon
juice, and spread over the cooled roulade base.
3 Scatter the arugula over the roulade, and roll up
as shown. Chill in the refrigerator for one hour.
Serve with fresh tomato sauce (page 121).

ROLLING UP A GRUYERE WITH RED PEPPER ROULADE

1 Spread the cottage cheese over the roulade base, leaving a border of about ½ inch all round to make the roulade easier to roll.

2 Cover with red peppers, then roll up the roulade, starting from a short side (this gives a thick roulade). Use the paper to help lift the base as you roll it.

3 Place the roulade with the seam underneath so it cannot unroll. Trim the ends and, if desired, sprinkle the top with freshly grated Parmesan.

Gruyère with red pepper roulade, served with quick herb sauce

CASHEW ROULADE WITH BROCCOLI

This very rich roulade, shown on page 37, is ideal as the centerpiece for a special dinner. Serves 6 as a starter, 4 as a main course.

INGREDIENTS

4 eggs
salt and freshly ground black pepper
1¼ cups roasted, unsalted cashews
2 cloves garlic
THE FILLING
1 quantity of freshly made hollandaise sauce (page 123)
1lb broccoli, trimmed and cut into small pieces
salt and freshly ground black pepper

PREPARATION

1 Preheat the oven to 400°F/200°C. Line a 9 x 13-inch shallow-sided baking sheet with waxed paper to extend slightly up the sides.
2 Break the eggs into a large bowl, add salt and black pepper, and beat until the mixture is thick and a trail left in it by the beaters remains visible for several seconds. This is done quickly using an electric beater; by hand it takes 5–10 minutes.
3 Put the cashews and garlic into a food processor or blender, and work until they are chopped finely but not oily and pulverized.
4 Stir two-thirds of the chopped nuts and garlic into the eggs, and then pour this mixture into the prepared pan, smoothing it to the edges. Bake until just firm and spongy in the center: 6–8 minutes.
5 Place a piece of waxed paper large enough for the roulade next to the oven, and sprinkle it with the remaining chopped nuts and garlic. Remove the roulade from the oven and place it, face down, onto the paper. Remove the waxed paper that was used to line the pan from the top.
6 Prepare the hollandaise as described on page 123.
7 Put the broccoli in a pan, pour in a little boiling water, cover and half-boil, half-steam until just tender and still bright green: 3 minutes. Drain.
8 Lightly spread the roulade base with some of the hollandaise sauce, then cover with an even layer of the broccoli. Roll up the roulade from one of the short sides (as shown on page 95).
9 Serve at once with the remaining hollandaise.

SPINACH ROULADE WITH CREAM CHEESE & PEPPERS

Illustrated on page 36, this roulade can be made in advance and reheated as described on page 94. Serves 6 as a starter, 4 as a main course.

INGREDIENTS

4 cups fresh young spinach leaves
1 tbsp butter
4 eggs, separated
freshly grated nutmeg
salt and freshly ground black pepper
4 tbsps grated Parmesan for coating
THE FILLING
1 large red pepper, quartered
1 cup cream cheese
a little milk

PREPARATION

1 Preheat the oven to 400°F/200°C. Line a 9 x 13-inch shallow-sided baking sheet with waxed paper to extend slightly up the sides.
2 Place the spinach in a pan with just the water that clings to its leaves after washing. Cook over moderate heat until tender: 7–10 minutes. Drain.
3 Put the spinach, butter, and egg yolks in a blender, and work until smooth. Transfer to a large bowl, and season with nutmeg, salt, and pepper.
4 In a separate bowl, whisk the egg whites until they are stiff. Fold the egg whites into the spinach mixture using a metal spoon, then pour the spinach and egg-white mixture into the prepared pan, smoothing it to the edges.
5 Sprinkle 2 tablespoons of the Parmesan cheese over the roulade. Bake the roulade until just firm and spongy in the center: 12–15 minutes.
6 Place a piece of waxed paper large enough for the roulade next to the oven, and sprinkle it with the remaining Parmesan. Remove the roulade from the oven and place it, face down, onto the paper. Remove the waxed paper that was used to line the pan from the top.
7 Roast and peel the pepper as shown on page 144. Remove the core and seeds, and cut into strips.
8 Beat the cream cheese with enough milk to make it spreadable, then cover the roulade with it. Arrange the red pepper over the top in widely spaced stripes, then roll up the roulade from one of the short sides (as shown on page 95).
9 Serve with yellow pepper sauce (page 120).

DEEP-FRIED BRIE WITH APRICOT SAUCE

Gooey Brie in a crisp coating of crumbs is delicious, particularly if it is accompanied by a sweet sauce such as apricot, or served with sweet mango chutney. Deep-fried Brie is most often served as a first course, but I prefer it as a main course with steamed vegetables or a leafy salad to balance its richness. It needs to be eaten immediately so is best made for only a small number of people, as here. Serves 3 as a starter, 2 as a main course.

INGREDIENTS

½lb wheel of Brie
1 egg, beaten
2 tbsps all-purpose flour, to coat
¾ cup dry bread crumbs, to coat
peanut oil for deep-frying
APRICOT SAUCE
½ cup apricot jam
lemon juice, to taste

PREPARATION

1 Cut the Brie into six even-sized portions. Dip the pieces of Brie first in the egg, then in the flour, then in the egg again, and finally in the bread crumbs, coating the pieces well so the cheese cannot ooze out during frying.
2 For the sauce, put the jam into a small saucepan with 2 tablespoons of water, place over low heat, and stir until the jam has melted. Add a squeeze or two of lemon juice to taste.
3 Fill a deep saucepan no more than half-full with oil and place over high heat. Once the oil reaches 350°F/180°C – when bubbles form on the handle of a wooden spoon stirred into the oil – it is ready for deep-frying.
4 Using a slotted spoon, place the portions of Brie in the hot oil (you may need to do two batches). The cheese should rise to the surface and start browning at once. As soon as the pieces are golden brown all over, remove with the slotted spoon, and place on a plate lined with crumpled paper towels. Quickly reheat the oil, and put in the second batch, if necessary. Serve at once, with the sauce.

DEEP-FRIED CREPE PARCELS WITH GOAT CHEESE FILLING

These are not as tricky to make as they might sound and the result is fabulous: a crisp coating of crumbs on a light crêpe enclosing a filling of melting goat cheese. I particularly enjoy the sharpness of goat cheese, but other cheeses can be used: Brie or Camembert, for example, or even blue cheese. I like something sweet with them, such as cranberry sauce, especially if it is around Christmas time. Serves 4.

INGREDIENTS

½ quantity of crêpe batter (page 149)
olive oil for cooking the crêpes
THE FILLING
1 cup firm goat cheese, such as Montrachet, cut into thin slices or small cubes, including the rind
THE COATING
2 eggs, beaten
1 cup fresh or dried bread crumbs, to coat
peanut oil for deep-frying

PREPARATION

1 Use the batter to make 4 large thin crêpes, about 8 inches in diameter.
2 Divide the goat cheese among the four crêpes, placing it in the center of each one. Fold the sides into the middle to make each into a rough square.
3 Dip the crêpe parcels first in the beaten egg, then in the bread crumbs, coating each one well.
4 Fill a deep saucepan no more than half-full with oil and place over high heat. Once the oil reaches 350°F/180°C – when bubbles form on the handle of a wooden spoon stirred into the oil – it is ready for deep-frying.
5 Using a slotted spoon, place the crêpe parcels in the hot oil, seamed-side up, and fry until brown and very crisp: 1–2 minutes. Turn them over, and briefly fry the other side. Remove the parcels using the slotted spoon, drain well on a plate lined with crumpled paper towels, and serve at once.

VEGETABLE FRITTATA

*More substantial than an omelette, a frittata consists of
a thick layer of lightly cooked vegetables set with egg
in a frying pan and served flat. Similar dishes are found
in Spain and the Middle East. Frittata is the Italian
version. Use any vegetables you like: asparagus and
artichoke heart are possibilities. Frittata needs only a
salad to accompany it, and can be served cold or warm.
Illustrated on pages 100–1. Serves 2.*

INGREDIENTS

½ cup baby carrots, trimmed
½ cup shallots, sliced
¾ cup zucchini, cut into ¼-inch slices
½ cup snow peas, trimmed
4 eggs
⅓ cup freshly grated Parmesan cheese
salt and freshly ground black pepper
2 tbsps olive oil

PREPARATION

1 Pour a little water, about 2 inches, into a
saucepan, and bring to a boil. Add the carrots and
shallots, cover, and cook for 2 minutes. Add the
zucchini and cook for another minute, then the
snow peas and cook for 1 minute more. Drain. The
vegetables should be tender but still crunchy.
2 Preheat the broiler to moderate.
3 Whisk the eggs lightly, add the Parmesan, and
season with a little salt and black pepper –
remembering that the cheese is fairly salty.
4 Heat the oil in a large frying pan over moderate
heat. Add the vegetables, using a spatula to
distribute them evenly around the pan, then pour
in the egg mixture, gently moving the vegetables
so the egg runs through them.
5 When the bottom of the frittata is set and
golden brown (1–2 minutes), put the pan under
the broiler until the top is set: 1–2 minutes. Slide
it onto a plate, and serve, cut in half or in wedges.

SPINACH TIMBALES

*Eggs, cream, and spinach, set in small timbale molds
or custard cups, make a light and delicious first course.
Illustrated on page 100. Serves 6 as a starter.*

INGREDIENTS

butter and grated Parmesan to coat the molds
1 tbsp butter
2 cups frozen chopped spinach
4 eggs
⅔ cup light cream
¼ cup heavy cream
freshly grated nutmeg
salt and freshly ground black pepper
torn frisée and carrot knots (page 145) to
garnish, optional

PREPARATION

1 Preheat the oven to 325°F/160°C. Line the
bases of 6 timbale molds or custard cups with
circles of waxed paper, grease with butter, and
dust with finely grated Parmesan.
2 Melt the butter in a large saucepan over
moderate heat, add the spinach, cover, and cook
until the spinach is tender: 3–4 minutes.
3 Separate two of the eggs. Place the yolks in a
bowl (reserve the whites to use in another recipe),
add the two whole eggs and the cream, and beat.
4 Pour the egg and cream mixture into the pan
with the spinach, mix well, and season with
nutmeg, salt, and black pepper. Divide among the
prepared molds. Bake in a bain-marie (see page
147) until set and firm to the touch and a skewer
inserted into the center comes out clean:
30–35 minutes.
5 Timbales can be served while still warm or
when cool. Cool slightly – or completely – then
loosen the sides with a knife and remove from the
molds. Garnish with a little torn frisée and carrot
knots, if desired, and serve.

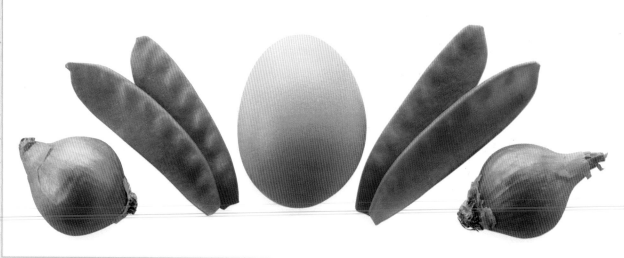

CLASSIC OMELETTE

Use the best organic eggs you can find for an excellent, highly satisfying result. Illustrated (with fresh herbs) on page 15. Serves 1.

INGREDIENTS

2 eggs
salt and freshly ground black pepper
1 tbsp butter

PREPARATION

1 Break the eggs into a bowl, and beat them lightly until yolks and whites have just combined. Season with salt and black pepper.
2 Place a small frying pan (about 6 inches across the base) over moderate heat and, when it is hot, add the butter. Swirl the butter around the pan without letting it brown. Pour in the eggs, tipping the pan so that it is evenly coated.
3 Using a fork, draw the edges of the egg toward the center and let the liquid egg run to the edges. Repeat until the omelette is almost set but still a little moist on top – it takes around a minute. Add the filling, fold the omelette into three (see page 148), serve, and eat at once.

SOUFFLED OMELETTE

Halfway between a soufflé and an omelette, this is far quicker to cook than a soufflé, and makes a change from a classic omelette. Serves 1.

INGREDIENTS

2 eggs, separated
2 tbsps cold water
salt and freshly ground black pepper
1 tbsp butter

PREPARATION

1 Preheat the broiler to moderate.
2 Put the egg yolks and water into a large bowl, season, and mix well.
3 In a separate greasefree bowl, whisk the egg whites until they stand in soft peaks.
4 Using a metal spoon, stir a little egg white into the yolks, then fold in the rest of the egg white.
5 Follow step 2 of the Classic Omelette, above.
6 After 1 – 2 minutes, when the bottom of the omelette is set and golden brown, put the pan under the broiler and brown the top: 1 – 2 minutes.
7 Slit the omelette open without cutting right through the base (this makes it foldable). Spoon your chosen filling over it, fold it and serve.

OMELETTE FILLINGS

A basic omelette, whether classic or souffléd, can have a wide variety of fillings, both sweet and savory. Each of the suggestions below is for a savory omelette, and serves 1. For sweet omelettes, add fruit or jam of your choice and, if desired, a dusting of powdered sugar. Have the filling ready to spoon onto the omelette the moment the omelette is cooked, then fold and serve.

ASPARAGUS Trim 2 – 4 asparagus spears and place in a frying pan. Pour in a little boiling water, cover and half-boil, half-steam them until tender: 3 – 4 minutes. Cut into 1-inch lengths.
RED PEPPER Roast and peel half a pepper (as shown on page 144) then slice the flesh.
MUSHROOM Slice 1¾ cups mushrooms – any type, or a mixture – and sauté in 1 tablespoon butter until tender and any liquid has evaporated: 5 – 15 minutes, depending on how much liquid they make. Season with salt and black pepper.
TRUFFLE Shave some black truffle onto the freshly cooked omelette and fold the omelette immediately.
RATATOUILLE Ratatouille (page 62) makes a good omelette filling: gently reheat about 2 generous tablespoons.
CHEESE Stir 2 tablespoons of grated cheese into the beaten eggs, then sprinkle 2 more tablespoons (of a different cheese, if desired) onto the freshly cooked omelette just before folding it. Gruyère and Parmesan are both delicious.
ARTICHOKE Allow 1 – 2 artichoke bases per person, prepared as shown on page 146, then sliced and gently tossed in a frying pan with 1 tablespoon of melted butter until tender.
ARUGULA This is a good filling if you like strong flavors. Use 1 bunch of leaves, added either raw or after being cooked in 2 teaspoons of olive oil in a frying pan for 1 – 2 minutes.
PEAS & MINT Cover ½ cup fresh or frozen peas with boiling water and cook until tender: about 2 minutes. Drain, and add a small piece of butter and 2 teaspoons of chopped fresh mint.

*Spinach timbale
(page 98)*

*Light bread rolls
(page 103)*

*Vegetable frittata
(page 98)*

BREAD, PIZZAS, & PASTRY

Fresh, home-baked breads and pastries are universally popular and are an important part of the vegetarian diet. Quiches and pies, in all their variety, make excellent, substantial main courses as well as delicious food for parties, picnics, and summer meals outdoors. Two of the dishes in this section, the Gougère and the Cashew and Tomato Pâté en Croûte, make stunning centerpieces for special dinners, while the easy yeast-based dough for light bread rolls and authentic pizza bases is the stuff of delicious everyday meals.

QUICK & EASY BROWN BREAD

This bread is made by the quick, one-rise method, which does not require any kneading. The dough is mixed, put into the pan to rise, then baked. Use fresh or dried yeast. I prefer fresh; it is pleasant to handle and seems to work more quickly. Two things are important: that the yeast is not stale (whether fresh or dried), and that the dough is not allowed to get hot until it goes into the oven. Makes two 1lb loaves.

INGREDIENTS

2 cups whole-wheat flour
2 tsps salt
*½oz fresh yeast **or** 2 tsps dried yeast*
1 tsp sugar
1⅓ cup tepid (not warm or hot) tepid water
butter or olive oil to grease the pan

PREPARATION

1 Pour the flour and salt into a large bowl, mix roughly with your fingers, and then leave in a warm place, such as an oven on very low, until the flour is warm to the touch. It is important that the flour does not get hot, it should be only warm.
2 If using fresh yeast, crumble it into a small bowl with the sugar and pour in ⅔ cup of the tepid water. If using dried yeast, put ⅔ cup of the water and the sugar into the bowl first, then sprinkle the yeast on top and stir.
3 Leave the yeast until it is frothy like the head on a glass of beer: about 5 minutes.

4 Generously grease two 3 x 5 x 9-inch loaf pans with butter or olive oil.
5 Add the yeast to the flour and enough of the remaining tepid water to make a fairly soft mixture that leaves the sides of the bowl clean. Add a little more tepid water if necessary.
6 Halve the dough. Flatten the dough into a rectangle and gently roll it up to fit the pan, then put it into the pan fold-side down. Push the dough down into the sides and corners to give a domed shape to the bread.
7 Cover the pans with plastic wrap or a clean dish cloth wrung out in hot water and leave in a warm place (such as near a heater or oven) until the dough is within ¼ inch of the top of the pan: about 30 minutes if the room is reasonably warm, longer – up to an hour even – if the room is cool.
8 Preheat the oven to 400°F/200°C.
9 Bake the bread until it is brown and firm to the touch: about 35 minutes. The bread should sound hollow when you slip it out of the pan and tap its base with your knuckles. To crisp the base and sides more, return the loaf to the oven for a few minutes after removing it from the pan. Cool the loaf on a wire rack.

VARIATION

For a lighter loaf, replace up to half the whole-wheat flour with all-purpose flour. Mix the flours roughly together in the bowl with your fingers, and then make the bread in exactly the same way as the all whole-wheat version.

LIGHT BREAD ROLLS

This olive oil dough requires a little kneading. The rolls can be any shape or size: see illustration on page 101.

INGREDIENTS

1½ cups all-purpose flour
1½ cups whole-wheat flour
½ tsp salt
*1 tbsp fresh yeast **or** 1 tsp dried yeast*
1 tsp sugar
1 cup tepid water
3 tbsps olive oil
butter or oil to grease the baking sheet
beaten egg or milk to glaze, optional
flour, poppy, or sesame seeds, or oat flakes to garnish, optional

PREPARATION

1 Pour the flours and salt into a large bowl, mix roughly together with your fingers and leave in a warm place until warm (not hot) to the touch.
2 If using fresh yeast, crumble it into a small bowl with the sugar, and pour in the tepid water. If using dried yeast, put the water and sugar into the bowl first, then sprinkle the yeast on top and stir.
3 Leave the yeast until it is frothy like the head on a glass of beer: about 5 minutes.
4 Add the oil to the flour, and pour in the yeast. Mix to a dough that leaves the sides of the bowl clean, then turn it out onto a clean work surface and knead for 5 – 10 minutes or until the dough feels smooth and silky. If sticky, add more flour.
5 Return the dough to the bowl and cover with plastic wrap or a clean dish cloth wrung out in hot water. Leave in a warm place until the dough has almost doubled in size: 30 minutes to an hour.
6 Punch down the dough with your fist, remove it from the bowl, and knead it briefly. Divide it into the required number of pieces and make the roll shapes (see right). Place well apart on a lightly greased baking sheet, cover with plastic wrap or a dish cloth wrung out in hot water, and leave in a warm place until doubled in size: 30–60 minutes or more. The rolls should look puffy.
7 Preheat the oven to 400°F/200°C.
8 If desired, glaze the rolls with egg or milk, and dust with flour or sprinkle with seeds or oat flakes. Bake until the rolls are lightly browned and sound hollow when tapped on the base: about 20 minutes. Cool on a wire rack.

ROLL SHAPES

Rolls can be made in small versions of traditional bread shapes (illustrated on page 101):
KNOT Divide the dough into eight pieces, roll each piece into a thin sausage shape, and tie into a loose knot.
COTTAGE Divide the dough into eight pieces and divide two of these into thirds, making six large pieces and six small. Gently roll under the palm of your hand into rounds, then place a small round on top of each large one, and make a hole down through the middle of both pieces using the handle of a wooden spoon.
CLOVER LEAF Divide the dough into about 18 small pieces. Roll gently into rounds and place them in threes, touching each other, on the baking sheet. Each group of three – each clover leaf – should be well separated from the next.
BRAID Divide the dough into three pieces. Divide each piece into three more pieces and roll into long thin sausage shapes. Pinch three ends together, loosely braid, then pinch the other ends together. Tuck the ends under to hold the braid firmly. Repeat to make two more.
BLOOMER Divide the dough into six pieces. Flatten each piece and roll it up like a jelly roll. Pull down on the ends and tuck them underneath to make the top round and smooth. After the dough has doubled in size and before it is glazed, cut two diagonal slits in the top.

PIZZA BASE

Use the same dough as for the light bread rolls, left. Makes one 12-inch round pizza base or four 6-inch bases. A selection of toppings appears on page 104.

PREPARATION

1 Follow steps 1 to 5 of the recipe on the left.
2 Lightly grease a pizza pan or baking sheet with butter or olive oil.
3 Punch down the dough with your fist, remove it from the bowl, and knead it briefly. Flatten it into a circle 12 inches in diameter or, to make individual pizzas, divide the dough into four pieces and flatten these into circles 6 inches in diameter. Place on the plate or baking sheet.
4 Arrange the toppings and bake the pizza or pizzas in the preheated oven, as described overleaf.

ASPARAGUS, ARUGULA, & PARMESAN PIZZA

Makes one 12-inch pizza.

INGREDIENTS

¾ cup asparagus tips
1 bunch arugula, lightly torn
1 x 12in pizza base (page 103), uncooked
olive oil, to taste
salt and freshly ground black pepper
⅔ cup Parmesan cheese, grated

PREPARATION

1 Preheat the oven to 400°F/200°C.
2 Cook the asparagus in boiling water until just tender: 2–3 minutes.
3 Sprinkle the arugula over the pizza base. Arrange the asparagus on top like the spokes of a wheel. Brush well with oil and season to taste.
4 Bake for 10 minutes. Add the cheese, return to the oven, and bake until crisp at the edges and light brown on top: 10 minutes. Serve at once.

ARTICHOKE, AVOCADO, & OYSTER MUSHROOM PIZZA

Makes one 12-inch pizza.

INGREDIENTS

2 tbsps olive oil
1 cup oyster mushrooms
1 quantity basic or fresh tomato sauce (page 121)
1 x 12in pizza base (page 103), uncooked
½ cup artichoke hearts, preserved in oil
1 ripe avocado
1 tbsp lemon juice
salt and freshly ground black pepper

PREPARATION

1 Preheat the oven to 400°F/200°C.
2 Warm the oil in a pan over moderate heat, add the mushrooms and fry for 5 minutes.
3 Spread the tomato sauce over the pizza base. Drain the artichoke hearts, reserving the oil, slice them and arrange with the mushrooms over the pizza. Brush well with the oil in which the artichokes were preserved. Bake for 15 minutes.
4 Halve the avocado, remove the peel and pit, and slice the flesh; sprinkle with the lemon juice.
5 Remove the pizza from the oven, arrange the avocado on top, season and return to the oven for 5 more minutes. Serve at once.

EGGPLANT, RED ONION, & GREEN OLIVE PIZZA

Makes one 12-inch pizza.

INGREDIENTS

1 large eggplant, cut into 1 x 2in strips
2 red onions, sliced
olive oil, to drizzle
1 x 12in pizza base (page 103), uncooked
1 cup large green olives, pitted
salt and freshly ground black pepper
⅔ cup goat cheese, sliced or diced, optional

PREPARATION

1 Preheat the oven to 400°F/200°C.
2 Place the eggplant and onion on the broiler pan or on a baking sheet. Drizzle oil over them, mix gently with your hands to spread the oil evenly, and place under the hot broiler until tender and lightly browned: about 10–15 minutes, turning with tongs and adding more oil as necessary.
3 Arrange the eggplant and onion over the pizza base, place the olives on top, and season well.
4 If adding cheese, bake without the cheese for 10 minutes, then add the cheese and return to the oven. Bake until crisp at the edges and light brown on top: 10 more minutes. Alternatively, bake without cheese until crisp at the edges and cooked in the middle: 20 minutes. Serve at once.

INDIVIDUAL PIZZAS

The pizza dough on page 103 makes four individual pizza bases of around 6 inch diameter. Some ingredients lend themselves particularly well to small pizzas: cherry tomatoes for example. Bake at the same temperature as the larger pizzas (400°F/200°C) but for less time: about 10–15 minutes.

CHERRY TOMATO PIZZAS Spread fresh tomato sauce (page 121) evenly over the bases. Thinly slice 2 cups red or yellow cherry tomatoes, arrange over the top and season well. Bake until the pizzas are crisp at the edges and cooked in the middle: about 10–15 minutes. Serve warm, strewn with fresh basil leaves.
MULTICOLORED PEPPERS PIZZAS Take 1 red, 1 yellow, and 1 green pepper, quarter, roast and peel them as shown on page 144, and cut the flesh into strips. Arrange over the bases, drizzle with olive oil if desired, and season well. Bake until crisp at the edges and cooked in the middle: about 10–15 minutes. Serve warm.

SAVORY QUICHES

These recipes make one 8-inch quiche or
four 4-inch small quiches. Illustrated on pages 30–1.

INGREDIENTS

THE QUICHE FILLING
a filling chosen from below
THE QUICHE CASES
1 x 8in shortcrust pastry shell **or**
4 x 4in shells, prebaked and
"waterproofed" as shown on page 151
THE CUSTARD
3 egg yolks
1 cup light cream
freshly grated nutmeg, optional
salt and freshly ground black pepper

PREPARATION

1 Preheat the oven to 325°F/160°C.
2 Prepare the filling ingredients as described below and divide among the prebaked shells.
3 Make the custard: in a small bowl, beat the egg yolks and the cream to combine them. Add the nutmeg, if desired, and a good seasoning of salt and black pepper. Pour the custard into a saucepan, place over gentle heat and cook, stirring with a wooden spoon, until it is thick enough to coat the back of the spoon.
4 Pour the custard over the ingredients in the pastry cases. Sprinkle with seeds or nuts if using. Place in the oven and bake until the filling is set and golden brown on top: 25–30 minutes.

—— *Quiche fillings* ——

LEEK & SESAME Slice 2 cups trimmed leeks. Cover and cook them slowly, stirring occasionally, in 2 tablespoons butter until tender and creamy: about 15 minutes. If the leeks produce liquid, uncover, turn up the heat, and boil it quickly away. Place the leeks in the pastry shell(s), season the custard with nutmeg and pour it over the leeks. Sprinkle 2 tablespoons of sesame seeds over the custard and bake. Serve hot, warm, or cold.

BLUE CHEESE & ONION WITH ALMONDS Cook a medium-sized onion, finely chopped, in 1 tablespoon olive oil until tender: 5 minutes. Crumble ¼ cup blue cheese, mix with the onion, and place in the pastry shell or shells. Pour the custard over the onion and cheese, sprinkle with 2 tablespoons of flaked almonds and bake. Serve hot, warm, or cold.

TINY QUICHES & TARTLETS

I usually prebake tiny pastry shells before adding the fillings, but I don't bother to waterproof them since they are so small. These amounts fill 6–8 tiny pastry shells. Illustrated on pages 30–1.

FETA, ARUGULA, & SUNDRIED TOMATO TARTLETS Mix 1 cup diced feta cheese and 12 roughly torn arugula leaves with 4 sundried tomatoes, cut into strips. Season with black pepper, divide evenly among 6–8 prebaked tartlet shells, and serve.

BLACK OLIVE & TOMATO TARTLETS Make a small quantity of tomato sauce (page 121) and spoon it into 6–8 prebaked tartlet shells. Cut 6–8 pitted black olives into strips and arrange over the sauce. Garnish with sprigs of oregano and serve.

MIXED PEPPER BARQUETTES Take 1 red and 1 yellow pepper, quarter, roast, and peel them as shown on page 144, and cut the flesh into strips. Arrange in 6–8 prebaked barquette shells, garnish with sprigs of basil, and serve.

CHERRY TOMATO BARQUETTES Preheat the oven to 325°F/160°C. Thinly slice 6 cherry tomatoes and arrange most of the slices in 6–8 prebaked barquette shells. Mix 1 egg yolk with 3 tablespoons of light cream and season with salt and black pepper. Spoon this mixture over the tomatoes in the shells, garnish with the remaining tomatoes and bake until the filling is set: 5–10 minutes. Serve warm or cold.

AVOCADO & SCALLION TINY QUICHES Preheat the oven to 325°F/160°C. Finely slice 2 small scallions and fry in a little olive oil until tender: 3 minutes. Mix 1 egg yolk with 8 tablespoons of light cream and season with salt and pepper. Peel, pit, and slice a small avocado, mix it with the scallion and divide among 6 tiny quiche shells. Pour in enough of the cream and egg mixture to fill the shells. Bake until the filling is set: 5–10 minutes. Serve warm or cold.

CARROT & CARDAMOM TINY QUICHES Preheat the oven to 325°F/160°C. Finely slice ⅔ cup baby carrots and boil them with a cardamom pod until tender: about 2 minutes. Drain the carrots and divide them among the small pastry shells. Split the cardamom pods, scoop out the seeds, and put them in a bowl with 1 egg and 8 tablespoons of cream. Mix the egg with the cream and season with salt and black pepper. Fill the cases with the mixture. Bake until the filling is set: 5–10 minutes. Serve warm or cold.

CASHEW & TOMATO PATE EN CROUTE

A moist cashew and tomato pâté with a coat of light, flaky puff pastry makes an excellent main course. It is made in two stages: the pâté is baked and cooled, then wrapped in pastry and baked again. Serves 4.

INGREDIENTS

butter, to coat pan
2 tbsps sundried tomato oil or olive oil
1 large onion, finely chopped
2 large cloves garlic, finely chopped
14oz can whole tomatoes, drained and chopped
12 sundried tomatoes in oil, finely chopped
1 cup cashews, finely chopped
zest of ½ lemon, finely chopped
1 tbsp chopped fresh basil
1 egg, beaten
salt and freshly ground black pepper
½lb frozen puff pastry or homemade quick flaky pastry (page 150)

PREPARATION

1 Preheat the oven to 350°F/180°C. Line a shallow 2 x 5 x 9-inch loaf pan with waxed paper and grease with butter.

2 Warm the oil in a saucepan over moderate heat, add the onion and garlic, cover, and cook for 5 minutes. Add the tomatoes and cook, uncovered, until any liquid has evaporated: about 3 minutes.

3 Remove from the heat and stir in the sundried tomatoes, cashews, lemon zest, basil, and all but 2 teaspoons of the egg (reserve for glazing). Season with salt and black pepper.

4 Spoon the mixture into the pan, smoothing the top. Bake until the center is firm to the touch: 45–60 minutes. Remove from the heat and allow to cool. Then turn the pâté out of the pan, wrap in foil or plastic wrap, and cool in the refrigerator.

The pâté can be made in advance and stored in the refrigerator for 2 – 3 days.

5 Preheat the oven to 400°F/200°C.

6 On a lightly floured board, roll out the puff pastry to a 12-inch square. Cut off the top third, measuring 12 x 4 inches.

7 Place the pâté on the smaller piece of pastry and drape the larger piece of pastry over the top, covering the pâté completely. Ease the pastry down the sides and press the edges firmly together at the bottom, sealing with water. Trim, make steam holes in the top, and glaze with the beaten egg. Bake until the pastry is crisp and puffed up: 25–30 minutes. Serve at once.

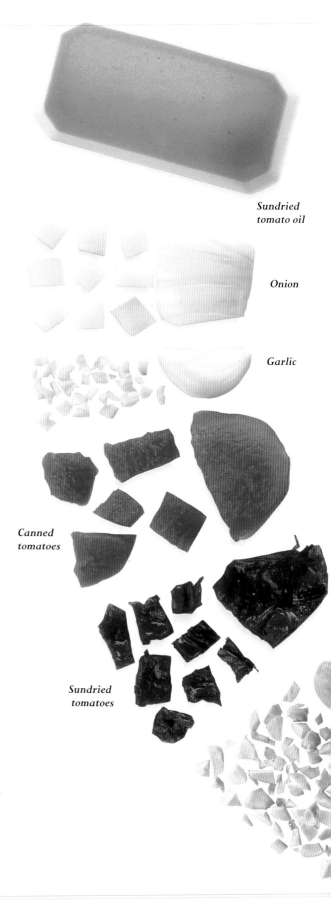

Sundried tomato oil

Onion

Garlic

Canned tomatoes

Sundried tomatoes

Cashews

Lemon zest

Basil

Beaten egg

Salt

Black pepper

Puff pastry

FLAKY LEEK & POTATO PIE

Here, satisfyingly creamy leeks and potatoes are baked under a flaky crust, which can be decorated according to your skill and ambition. Serves 4.

INGREDIENTS

3 large potatoes, thinly sliced
4 medium trimmed leeks, sliced
2 tbsps butter
1 large onion, finely chopped
2 tbsps chopped fresh chives
2 tbsps chopped fresh flat-leaf parsley
1¾ cup crème fraîche
freshly grated nutmeg
salt and freshly ground black pepper
½lb frozen puff pastry or homemade quick flaky pastry (page 150)
beaten egg to glaze, optional

PREPARATION

1 Cook the potatoes in boiling water until just tender: 8–10 minutes. In another pan, cook the leeks in boiling water until just tender: 8–10 minutes. Drain. (The water from both vegetables makes good stock.)

2 Melt the butter in a large saucepan over low heat, add the onion, cover, and cook until tender: about 10 minutes.

3 Remove the onion from the heat and add the potatoes, leeks, herbs, and crème fraîche. Mix well, season with nutmeg, salt and black pepper, and leave to cool.

4 Preheat the oven to 400°F/200°C.

5 Take a 10-inch pie pan. Roll out the pastry so that it is larger all around than the pie pan. Cut around the pie pan to make the top crust, and then cut around this, 1 inch from the pan, to make the pie rim. Set these, and any trimmings, aside.

6 Spoon the filling into the pie pan. It should fill it generously and form a rounded dome.

7 Fit the pastry rim on the edge of the pie pan, pleating it if necessary, brush with cold water, and position the top crust on top to cover the whole pan. Press the edges firmly together to seal the pie, then flute and scallop the pie rim as shown on page 151. Make a steam hole in the center. Decorate the pie with pastry trimmings, sticking them on with cold water, then brush with beaten egg if desired.

8 Bake until puffed up and golden brown: 35–40 minutes. Serve at once.

GRUYERE GOUGERE

A gougère – a circle of golden, light, cheese-enriched choux pastry filled with vegetables cooked in red wine – makes a mouthwatering centerpiece for a meal. Other fillings can be good too: try the vegetable recipes on page 62. Serves 4.

INGREDIENTS

THE GOUGERE
4 tbsps butter, plus extra to coat the dish
¾ cup all-purpose flour
2 eggs
⅔ cup Gruyère cheese, grated
salt and freshly ground pepper
THE FILLING
1 tbsp butter
1 tbsp olive oil
1 large onion, sliced
4 cloves garlic, chopped
1 cup baby carrots
1½ cups baby button mushrooms
1 bay leaf
1 sprig of rosemary
1¼ cup red wine
chopped fresh flat-leaf parsley, to garnish

PREPARATION

1 Preheat the oven to 400°F/200°C.

2 Put the butter into a medium saucepan with ⅔ cup of cold water and heat gently to melt the butter and bring the water to a boil.

3 Remove from the heat and sift in the flour. Stir vigorously, then return to the heat, and keep stirring until the mixture leaves the sides of the pan. Remove from the heat once again.

4 Add the eggs and beat the mixture with a wooden spoon until it becomes smooth and glossy: 2–3 minutes. Stir in two-thirds of the cheese and season well.

5 Lightly grease a 12-inch ovenproof plate or dish with butter and place spoonfuls of the mixture on it in a ring. Sprinkle the rest of the cheese on top. Bake until it has risen, looks golden, and is firm to the touch: about 35 minutes.

6 Meanwhile, make the filling. Melt half the butter with the oil in a large pan over moderate heat, add the onion, and fry for 5 minutes. Add the garlic, carrots, mushrooms, and herbs, and fry for 5 minutes longer, then reduce the heat.

7 Pour in the wine and cook until it has reduced by half: about 20 minutes. Discard the herbs. Season and add the rest of the butter.

8 Spoon the vegetables into the center of the gougère, sprinkle with parsley, and serve at once.

ASPARAGUS PHYLLO FLOWERS

Makes 12. Illustrated on page 18.

INGREDIENTS

phyllo pastry (see page 150 for tips on using it)
melted butter for brushing
8 asparagus spears
1 quantity of hollandaise sauce (page 123)

PREPARATION

1 Preheat the oven to 400°F/200°C.
2 You need a muffin pan and, for each flower, two squares of phyllo pastry that are slightly bigger than the cup-shaped hollows. Cut the phyllo into squares.
3 Brush a little melted butter into each hollow and put in one square of phyllo pastry, then place another on top slightly askew, so there are eight points sticking up. Brush again with melted butter for an extra-rich result.
3 Continue until the pan is full. Bake the flowers until golden and crisp: about 5 minutes. Remove from the oven and leave to cool.
4 Cut the asparagus spears in three and boil briefly in salted boiling water until tender: about 3 minutes. Allow to cool.
5 Place the flowers on a serving platter, fill each one with a generous amount of hollandaise sauce and arrange two asparagus tips in it. Serve at once.

VARIATION

BROCCOLI AND TOMATO PHYLLO FLOWERS
Arrange lightly cooked broccoli florets and strips of fresh tomato in hollandaise-filled flowers.

SPRING ROLLS

Makes 12. Illustrated on page 18.

INGREDIENTS

2 tbsps olive oil
1 medium-sized onion, finely chopped
1 green pepper, cored, seeded, and finely chopped
2 cups button mushrooms, sliced or chopped
1¼ cups bean sprouts
1 tbsp soy sauce
freshly ground black pepper
phyllo pastry (see page 150 for tips on using it)
melted butter for brushing

PREPARATION

1 Warm the oil in a large saucepan over moderate heat, add the onion and pepper, cover, and cook until tender: about 10 minutes.
2 Add the mushrooms and bean sprouts and cook uncovered for 2–3 minutes longer. Remove from the heat, add the soy sauce, season with black pepper, and leave to cool.
3 Preheat the oven to 400°F/200°C.
4 Fold a sheet of phyllo pastry in half lengthways. Spoon some mixture onto the narrow end of the strip of pastry, make a ½-inch fold like a hem down each side, then roll the package up. Brush with melted butter and place on a baking sheet. Repeat until the filling is used up.
5 Bake until golden and crisp on both sides: after about 20 minutes on one side, turn over and bake for 10–15 minutes on the other. Serve at once or recrisp in a warm oven later.

LEEK PARCELS

Makes 8. Illustrated on page 18.

INGREDIENTS

2 large potatoes, finely diced
3 medium trimmed leeks, finely sliced
⅔ cup light cream
2 tbsps chopped fresh flat-leaf parsley
salt and freshly ground black pepper
phyllo pastry (see page 150 for tips on using it)
melted butter for brushing

PREPARATION

1 Cook the potatoes and leeks in boiling water in separate pans until just tender: 5–6 minutes each. Drain. (The water makes good stock.)
2 Put the potatoes and leeks into a bowl and pour in the cream, adding a little at a time so that you can prevent the mixture from becoming too runny. Stir in the flat-leaf parsley, season with salt and black pepper, and mix well.
3 Preheat the oven to 400°F/200°C.
4 Cut a sheet of phyllo pastry in half lengthwise and arrange one piece on top of the other in a cross shape. Place some filling in the center and fold over the four flaps to make a parcel. Brush with melted butter and place on a baking sheet. Repeat until the filling is used up.
5 Bake until golden and crisp on both sides: after about 20 minutes on one side, turn them over and bake for 10–15 minutes longer on the other. Serve at once or recrisp in a warm oven later.

SPICED VEGETABLE TRIANGLES

Makes 8. Illustrated on page 19.

INGREDIENTS

1 tbsp olive oil
1 medium-sized onion, finely chopped
½ tsp grated fresh ginger
½ tsp cumin seeds
½ tsp ground coriander
3½oz finely diced potato
3½oz finely diced carrot
3½oz frozen peas
2 tbsps chopped fresh cilantro
salt and freshly ground black pepper
phyllo pastry (see page 150 for tips on using it)
melted butter for brushing

PREPARATION

1 Warm the oil in a large pan over moderate heat, add the onion, cover, and cook until tender: 5 minutes. Add the spices, potato, and carrot, cover, and cook until the vegetables are tender: about 10 minutes. Stir occasionally, and add a tablespoon or so of water if the mixture sticks.
2 Put in the frozen peas and stir until they are thawed. Add the fresh cilantro and seasoning.
3 Preheat the oven to 400°F/200°C.
4 Cut a sheet of phyllo pastry lengthwise into two strips. Spoon filling onto the top edge of one strip and make a triangle as shown above. Brush with melted butter, place on a baking sheet, and repeat.
5 Bake until golden and crisp: about 15 minutes.

MONEY BAGS

Makes 12. Illustrated on page 19.

INGREDIENTS

½ cup ricotta cheese
⅓ cup freshly grated Parmesan cheese
phyllo pastry (see page 150 for tips on using it)
melted butter for brushing

PREPARATION

1 Preheat the oven to 400°F/200°C.
2 Mix together the ricotta and Parmesan cheese.
3 Cut the phyllo into 5-inch squares. Brush one square with melted butter and place another on top slightly askew. Spoon filling onto the middle and gather up the edges, pressing them together to make a pouch. Brush with melted butter, place on a baking sheet, and repeat.
4 Bake until golden and crisp: about 5 minutes.

MAKING A PHYLLO TRIANGLE

1 *Place the filling at the top of the pastry strip and draw one corner diagonally across to make a triangle.*

LITTLE GREEK PIES

Makes 8. Illustrated on page 19.

INGREDIENTS

2 cups tender spinach leaves
1 tbsp olive oil
1 medium-sized onion, finely chopped
½ tsp fennel seeds
½ cup feta cheese, crumbled or diced
salt and freshly ground black pepper
phyllo pastry (see page 150 for tips on using it)
melted butter for brushing

PREPARATION

1 Place the spinach in a pan with just the water clinging to its leaves after washing. Cook over a medium heat until wilted: about 7 minutes. Drain, transfer to a bowl, and chop well.
2 Warm the oil in a pan over moderate heat, add the onion, cover, and cook for 5 minutes. Add the fennel seeds and cook for 1–2 minutes longer.
3 Add the onion mixture and the feta cheese to the spinach. Season lightly with salt (feta cheese is rather salty) and black pepper, mix thoroughly and allow to cool.
4 Preheat the oven to 400°F/200°C.
5 Cut a sheet of phyllo pastry lengthwise into two strips. Spoon filling onto the top edge of one strip and make a triangle as shown above. Brush with melted butter, place on a baking sheet, and repeat.
6 Bake until golden and crisp: about 10 minutes.

 Phyllo parcels and pies are best served straight from the oven. If made in advance, they can be recrisped in a warm oven before serving.

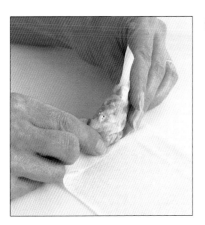

2 Begin to wrap the filling into a parcel by carefully folding the triangle over at its base.

3 Continue to wrap the parcel until you get to the end of the strip. Trim off any spare pastry.

4 Brush with melted butter, making sure the edges of the triangle are well sealed. Place on a baking sheet.

Greek pies

GRAINS & LEGUMES

M any of the world's most celebrated dishes have as their base
one of the rich variety of grains and legumes available.
Their international use is reflected in the classic recipes here,
ranging from India's dal and Italy's risotto to "new wave" red bean
roulade and a saffron-infused vegetable version of Spain's paella.

RICE & EGGPLANT MOLD

*This looks impressive made in a large 1 quart mold,
and can also be made in six individual molds
such as custard cups. Serves 6.*

INGREDIENTS

1¼ cups brown rice
2 medium-sized eggplants, thinly sliced
2 tbsps olive oil, plus extra for
frying the eggplants and greasing the mold
1 large onion, chopped
1 red pepper, seeded, and chopped
2 cloves garlic, chopped
¼ tsp chili powder
2 large tomatoes, peeled and chopped
¼ cup chopped fresh flat-leaf parsley
salt and freshly ground black pepper
sprigs of fresh basil, to garnish

PREPARATION

1 First, cook the rice (page 152). Remove from
the heat, but leave the pan covered.
2 Prepare the eggplants. For a rich result, shallow
fry in olive oil until tender: 2–3 minutes each
side. Drain well on paper towels to remove excess
oil. For a less rich result, steam until just tender:
4–5 minutes. Put to one side.
3 Warm 2 tablespoons of olive oil over moderate
heat, add the onion and red pepper, cover, and
cook for 10 minutes. Add the garlic, chili powder,
and tomatoes, and cook, uncovered, until the
tomatoes have reduced: about 10 minutes.
4 Add the tomato mixture to the rice, along with
the parsley, and salt and black pepper. Mix well.
5 Brush the mold(s) with oil, and arrange the
eggplant to cover the surface completely. Spoon in
the rice mixture, pressing down firmly, and top
with any remaining eggplant slices.
6 Refrigerate if serving chilled, or cover with
foil, and transfer to a warm oven. Remove from
the mold(s), and serve, garnished with basil.

MIXED VEGETABLE PILAU

*This is a spiced rice dish that goes well with Bombay
Potatoes and Spiced Okra (page 86). Serves 4.*

INGREDIENTS

3 tbsps olive oil
1 medium-sized onion, chopped
3–4 medium carrots, diced
2 cloves garlic, chopped
1 bay leaf
½ cinnamon stick
4 cardamom pods, crushed
2 tsps cumin seeds
1½ cups long-grain brown or white rice
salt
1 cup frozen peas, thawed
½lb button mushrooms, sliced
freshly ground black pepper
chopped fresh cilantro, to garnish

PREPARATION

1 Warm 2 tablespoons of the oil in a large
saucepan over moderate heat, add the onion and
carrots, cover, and cook for 10 minutes. Stir in
the garlic, bay leaf, and spices.
2 Add the rice, 1 quart of water, and 1 teaspoon
of salt. Bring to a boil, then reduce the heat,
cover, and cook until the rice is done: about
40 minutes for brown rice, 20 for white. The dish
should be moist but not runny when cooked.
3 Place the peas on top of the rice, cover the pan,
and take it off the heat. Let it stand for 10 minutes
to finish cooking in its own heat.
4 Meanwhile, fry the mushrooms in the
remaining oil until tender and any liquid they
produce has evaporated: 5–10 minutes.
5 Add the mushrooms to the rice mixture. Stir
gently with a wooden fork to combine all the
ingredients, removing and discarding the bay leaf
and cinnamon stick if desired. Season to taste and
serve, sprinkled with cilantro.

Vegetable Paella

This is a vegetable version of the classic Spanish dish. Vary the vegetables as much as you like, but put quick-cooking ones, such as zucchini, on top of the rice toward the end of the cooking time. Traditionally this dish is flavored and colored with saffron. Turmeric, which is similar in color, can be used instead. Serves 4.

INGREDIENTS

*6 saffron threads **or** ¼tsp turmeric (see note above)*
¼ cup olive oil
2 large onions, chopped
3–4 medium carrots, sliced
1 green and 1 red pepper, seeded, and sliced
1 eggplant, diced
2 cloves garlic, chopped
1½ cups short-grain rice
14oz can whole peeled tomatoes,
coarsely chopped, with juice
salt and freshly ground black pepper
chopped fresh flat-leaf parsley, to serve

PREPARATION

1 If you are using saffron, put the threads into a pitcher and fill with 1⅓ cups of boiling water. Leave to soak for approximately 20 minutes.
2 Warm the olive oil in a large saucepan over moderate heat, add the onion, cover, and cook until tender: about 10 minutes.
3 Stir in the carrots, peppers, eggplant, garlic, and rice, and keep stirring over the heat until the rice becomes translucent: 3–4 minutes.
4 Pour in the tomatoes. Add the saffron together with its soaking water, or the turmeric along with 1⅓ cups of boiling water, and stir well to mix. Season with plenty of salt – about 2 teaspoons – and some black pepper.
5 Bring the mixture to a boil, then reduce the heat, and simmer, covered, until the rice is cooked and the water absorbed: about 20 minutes. Take the paella off the heat, and leave to stand, still covered, for 10 minutes. Check the seasoning and serve, sprinkled with parsley.

PORCINI RISOTTO

Italian dried mushrooms — porcini — give this risotto its distinctive flavor. Other ingredients can be added too: baby peas and whole baby artichokes are good mixed into the risotto at the end of the cooking time, or you can replace ⅔ of a cup of water with the same volume of dry white wine, added at step 3 along with the porcini. The dish should be creamy and moist but with some bite still left in the grains of rice. Italian arborio rice gives the best result. Serves 4.

INGREDIENTS

½ oz dried porcini
¼ cup olive oil
2 large onions, chopped
2 garlic cloves, chopped
1½ cups arborio or risotto rice
10 oz oyster mushrooms
1 tbsp butter
freshly grated nutmeg
salt and freshly ground black pepper
chopped fresh flat-leaf parsley, to serve

PREPARATION

1 Put the porcini into a small bowl and cover with about 1½ cups of boiling water. Leave to soak.
2 Warm 3 tablespoons of the oil in a large saucepan over moderate heat, add the onions, cover, and cook for 10 minutes. Add the garlic and rice and stir over the heat for a few minutes until the rice is well coated in oil and looks translucent.
3 Drain the porcini through a strainer lined with a paper towel to catch any grit, reserving the liquid. Add enough water to the soaking liquid to make a quart and pour into a small saucepan. Set over moderate heat next to the large saucepan.
4 Chop the porcini, and stir into the rice. Add the porcini liquid, a ladleful at a time, stirring each addition and allowing it to become absorbed before adding the next. Continue until the risotto is creamy and the rice *al dente*: about 20 minutes.
5 Meanwhile, fry the oyster mushrooms in the remaining oil and the butter until they are tender: about 4 minutes. Stir the mushrooms gently into the rice mixture. Add nutmeg, salt, and black pepper, and serve, sprinkled with parsley.

BULGUR & PINENUT PILAF

This light dish of bulgur wheat, nuts, and dried fruit is a popular Turkish meal. Bulgur wheat, which is quicker to cook than rice, makes a good accompaniment in place of rice. Serves 4.

INGREDIENTS

1 tbsp butter
1 tbsp olive oil
1 medium-sized onion, chopped
2 garlic cloves, chopped
1⅓ cups bulgur wheat
1 tsp sea salt
½ cup pinenuts
⅓ cup raisins
chopped fresh flat-leaf parsley, to serve
freshly ground black pepper

PREPARATION

1 Melt the butter with the oil in a large saucepan over moderate heat, add the onion, cover, and cook for 5 minutes.
2 Stir in the garlic and bulgur wheat, coating the wheat with the oil and onion, then pour in 2½ cups of boiling water and the salt. Return to a boil, cover, and cook until the bulgur wheat is tender and the water absorbed: about 15 minutes.
3 Meanwhile, spread the pinenuts on a cookie sheet and lightly toast under a hot broiler, shaking the pan to move them around. They toast quickly.
4 Add the nuts, raisins, and parsley to the bulgur wheat, forking them through gently. Taste, season with black pepper, and serve.

WILD RICE

The colors and textures of wild rice mixed with brown and basmati rice make an attractive side dish. Serves 4.

INGREDIENTS

½ cup brown rice
¼ cup wild rice
¼ tsp sea salt
¼ cup basmati rice

PREPARATION

1 Put the brown and wild rice in a saucepan with 2 cups of water and the salt. Bring to a boil, cover, reduce the heat, and cook until the rice is tender and the water absorbed: 40 minutes.
2 Cook the basmati rice in plenty of boiling water: 10 minutes. Drain; rinse with hot water.
3 Mix the rices together with a fork.

LEMON RICE

Refreshing to look at as well as to eat, lemon rice goes well with many dishes. Serves 4.

INGREDIENTS

1 cup long-grain brown or white rice, rinsed
½ tsp turmeric
¼ tsp sea salt
juice and finely sliced zest of ½ lemon
freshly ground black pepper

PREPARATION

1 Put the rice in a saucepan with 2½ cups of water, the turmeric, and salt. Bring to a boil.
2 Turn the heat down to very low, cover, and cook until the rice is tender and the water absorbed: 40 minutes for brown rice, 20 for white.
3 Add the lemon juice and zest and stir with a fork. Season to taste with black pepper.

HERB RICE

This summery rice goes well with braised vegetable dishes such as ratatouille. It is also good cold. Serves 4.

INGREDIENTS

1 cup long-grain brown or white rice, rinsed
¼ tsp sea salt
6 tbsps finely chopped fresh herbs, such as parsley, mint, chives, tarragon
freshly ground black pepper

PREPARATION

1 Put the rice in a saucepan with 2½ cups of water and the salt. Bring to a boil.
2 Turn the heat down to very low, cover, and cook until the rice is tender and the water absorbed: 40 minutes for brown rice, 20 for white.
3 Add the herbs and stir with a fork. Season to taste with black pepper.

COCONUT RICE

This has a smooth texture and a slightly sweet flavor that goes well with spiced vegetable dishes. Serves 4.

INGREDIENTS

1 cup long-grain brown or white rice, rinsed
¼ tsp sea salt
¼ cup coconut milk
freshly ground black pepper

PREPARATION

1 Put the rice in a saucepan with 2½ cups of water and the salt. Bring to a boil.
2 Add the coconut, turn the heat down to very low, cover, and cook until the rice is tender and the water absorbed: 40 minutes for brown rice, 20 for white.
3 Stir gently with a fork. Season to taste with black pepper.

SPICED RICE

Slender basmati rice is available in brown and white varieties; I prefer the nutty taste of brown. Serves 4.

INGREDIENTS

1 cup basmati rice, rinsed
1 bay leaf
½ cinnamon stick, 2–3 crushed cardamom pods, 1 tsp cumin seeds
¼ tsp sea salt
freshly ground black pepper

PREPARATION

1 Put the rice in a saucepan with 2½ cups of water, the bay leaf, spices, and salt. Bring to a boil.
2 Turn the heat down to very low, cover, and cook until the rice is tender and the water absorbed: 20 minutes for brown rice, 10–12 for white.
3 Season to taste with black pepper.

RED BEAN ROULADE WITH SOUR CREAM FILLING

The base for this unusual roulade contains neither eggs nor cheese. For a vegan version, replace the cream and cottage cheese filling with avocado sauce (page 123). Indeed, avocado sauce goes so well with red beans that it makes the perfect sauce, whatever the filling. (Illustrated on page 37.) Serves 6 as a starter, 4 as a main course.

INGREDIENTS

2 tbsps olive oil
1 medium-sized onion, chopped
2 red peppers, cored, seeded, and chopped
14oz can whole peeled tomatoes,
coarsely chopped, with their juice
½ tsp chili powder
2 x 14oz cans red kidney beans, drained
2 cups fresh white bread crumbs
salt and freshly ground black pepper

THE FILLING

1 cup cottage cheese or farmer's cheese
⅔ cup sour cream
3 tbsps chopped fresh cilantro

PREPARATION

1 Preheat the oven to 400°F/200°C. Line a 9 x 13-inch jelly roll pan with waxed paper to extend slightly up the sides.
2 Warm the oil in a large saucepan over moderate heat, add the onion, cover, and cook until tender: 5 minutes. Add the peppers, cover, and cook for 5 minutes longer.
3 Add the tomatoes and chili powder and cook, uncovered, until the excess liquid evaporates and the mixture is thick: about 15 minutes.
4 Put the beans into a food processor or blender with the tomato mixture and bread crumbs. Season, then work to a fairly coarse consistency.
5 Spoon the mixture into the pan, spreading it evenly into the corners and leveling the top. Bake in the preheated oven until the center is firm: 10–15 minutes.
6 Make the filling by beating together the cottage cheese, sour cream, and cilantro.
7 Place a piece of waxed paper, large enough for the roulade, next to the oven. Remove the roulade from the oven and place it, face down, onto the paper. Remove the waxed paper that was used to line the pan from the top.
8 Spread the filling over the roulade, then gently roll it up from one of the narrow edges, pressing it together as you go. Carefully slice the roulade, and serve it on individual plates. It is fragile and may need reshaping with a palette knife.

RED BEAN CHILI

A vegetarian chili is one of the quickest and easiest dishes to make, and many people enjoy it. It is ideal for feeding a crowd, too: just double or triple the quantities. At the end of the cooking time, I like to mash the beans a little to make the mixture thick and then serve it with rice, bread, or potatoes. Serves 4.

INGREDIENTS

¼ cup olive oil
2 medium-sized onions, chopped
2 red or green peppers, cored, seeded, and chopped
2 fresh green chilis, seeded, and finely chopped
2 cloves garlic, chopped
1 tbsp cumin seeds
2 x 14oz cans whole peeled tomatoes,
coarsely chopped, with juice
2 x 14oz cans red kidney beans
salt and freshly ground black pepper

PREPARATION

1 Warm the oil in a large saucepan over moderate heat, add the onion, cover, and cook until tender: 5 minutes. Add the peppers, cover, and cook for 5 minutes longer.
2 Add the chilis, garlic, and cumin seeds and stir, then pour in the tomatoes.
3 Drain the beans, reserving the liquid. Add enough water to the liquid to make ⅔ cup, and pour the beans and liquid into the pan.
4 Bring to a boil, then cover, reduce the heat, and cook gently until the mixture is heated through and looks thick: 15–20 minutes. Season to taste with salt and black pepper, and serve.

SPINACH DAL

This dish goes well with Bombay Potatoes (page 86), Spiced Rice (page 115), and Spiced Okra (page 86). Serves 4 as a side dish.

INGREDIENTS

2 tbsps olive oil
2 medium-sized onions, chopped
2 fresh green chili peppers, seeded, and finely chopped
2 cloves garlic, chopped
2 tsps ground cumin
¼ tsp turmeric
3–4 cardamom pods, crushed
½ cup red lentils
4 cups tender spinach leaves
salt and freshly ground black pepper

PREPARATION

1 Warm the oil in a large saucepan over moderate heat, add the onion, cover, and cook for 10 minutes. Stir in the chilis, garlic, cumin, turmeric, and cardamom, and cook for 1 minute.
2 Add the lentils and 2 cups of water. Bring to a boil, then reduce the heat, cover, and cook until the lentils are soft and pale: 20–30 minutes. Remove the cardamon pods.
3 When the lentils are almost ready, cook the spinach. Place it in a saucepan with just the water clinging to its leaves after washing. Cook over moderately high heat until collapsed and much reduced in size: about 7 minutes. Drain well.
4 Mix the spinach into the lentil mixture and season well. Serve at once, or reheat later.

POLENTA

Coarse or fine cornmeal – polenta – can be pressed into flat slices, fried in olive oil, and served with fresh tomato sauce (page 121) or tomato salad. Serves 4 as a side dish.

INGREDIENTS

1½ cups polenta or cornmeal, coarse or fine grain
1 tbsp salt
olive oil for shallow frying
Parmesan cheese and lemon wedges to serve, optional

PREPARATION

1 Pour the polenta and salt into a medium-sized saucepan with 1 quart of cold water and mix to a smooth paste. Place over moderate heat, and stir gently until the mixture boils. Reduce the heat, and cook until the polenta is thick and comes away from the sides of the pan: about 30 minutes.

2 Spread the mixture on a baking sheet to just under a ½-inch thickness, and leave to cool.
3 Heat a little olive oil in a frying pan. Cut the polenta into slices, and fry on both sides until crisp and golden. Drain on paper towels. Do not cover the slices – this makes them soggy – but keep them warm in the oven if necessary.
4 Serve on a warmed dish, with grated Parmesan on top and lemon wedges on the side if desired.

FALAFEL

This is a quick and easy recipe for falafel, especially if you have a food processor. To make a light meal, serve with salad, pita bread, and yogurt mixed with fresh cilantro or dill. Serves 4 as a side dish or snack.

INGREDIENTS

14oz can chickpeas, drained
1 shallot or small onion
1 clove garlic, chopped
½ tsp ground cumin
pinch of cayenne pepper or chili powder
1 egg, beaten
1 tbsp all-purpose flour, a pinch of baking soda,
and a pinch of salt
salt and freshly ground black pepper
peanut oil for deep frying
olive oil and lemon juice, to serve

PREPARATION

1 Put the chickpeas and the shallot or onion into a food processor and purée. Transfer to a bowl. Alternatively, put the chickpeas into a bowl, mash well, and then grate the onion into them.
2 Add the garlic, ground cumin, cayenne pepper or chili powder, egg, and flour, and combine into a paste that just holds together. Season to taste with salt and black pepper.
3 Pour about 3 inches of oil into a saucepan, and place over high heat. Once the oil reaches 350°F/180°C – when bubbles form on the handle of a wooden spoon dipped into the oil – it is ready.
4 With floured hands, quickly form small amounts of the chickpea mixture into even rounds. Use a slotted spoon to drop several at a time into the hot oil. Fry until the submerged part is crisp – about 1 minute – then turn them over with the slotted spoon and crisp the other side.
5 Drain the falafel on paper towels. Do not cover – this makes them soggy – but keep them warm in the oven if necessary.
6 Continue until all the falafel are done. Serve warm, moistened with olive oil and lemon juice.

CARROT, ZUCCHINI, & APRICOT COUSCOUS

The term "couscous" refers both to the small round semolina-like grains themselves and to the complete dish of cooked grains and stew. The stew varies but is usually lightly spiced and contains chickpeas and perhaps some dried fruit. Serve it with small bowls of relishes with contrasting flavors: diced cucumber, creamy yogurt, toasted almonds, washed and plumped raisins, and store-bought harissa, a hot pepper sauce. Serves 4.

INGREDIENTS

3 tbsps peanut oil
1 large onion, chopped
3 – 4 medium carrots, sliced
2 cloves garlic, chopped
1 tsp ground ginger
¼ tsp freshly ground white or black pepper
¼ tsp ground cinnamon
½ cup dried apricots, sliced
14oz can chickpeas, drained
2 medium-sized zucchini, sliced
1½ tsps salt
2 cups couscous
3 tbsps butter
chopped flat-leaf parsley, to serve

PREPARATION

1 Heat 2 tablespoons of the oil in a large pan, add the onion and carrots, cover, and cook over moderate heat for about 10 minutes.

2 Stir the garlic, ground ginger, white or black pepper, and cinnamon into the onion and carrots, cover, and cook for about 2 minutes.

3 Add the apricots and chickpeas to the pan and pour in 1 quart of water. Bring to a boil, and simmer until the carrots and apricots are tender and the liquid thickens a little: about 20 minutes.

4 Drop in the zucchini, cover, and cook until tender: about 10 minutes.

5 Meanwhile, prepare the couscous. Put the remaining tablespoon of oil into a large saucepan, pour in 1½ cups of water and 1½ teaspoons of salt, and place over high heat. When the water is boiling, take it off the heat, pour in the couscous grain and leave to swell for 2 minutes. Then add the butter, place over low heat, and stir with a fork until heated through: 3 minutes.

6 Check the seasoning of the stew, sprinkle with parsley, and serve with the couscous.

Ground cinnamon

White pepper

Ground ginger

Garlic

Carrot

Onion

Peanut oil

Dried apricots

Chickpeas

Zucchini

Salt

Couscous

Butter

Flat-leaf parsley

SAUCES

A well-chosen sauce adds the finishing touch to both appetizers and main course dishes. Sauces can look stunning, see the terrines on pages 12–13, for example, and provide just the right touch of piquancy, creaminess, or even sweetness to set off a dish perfectly. In this section, you will find many sauces to enhance your meals. Most are highly versatile and can be made in advance, and all are guaranteed to impress.

PEPPER SAUCE

I like this best made with red peppers, though it works with any color pepper. It is a bright, mild but delicious sauce that complements many vegetarian dishes. You can add extra flavorings, as suggested, and use olive oil or butter, depending on the flavor you want. Serves 4.

INGREDIENTS

1 large pepper, cored, and seeded
1¼ cups homemade vegetable stock or water
*1 clove garlic, peeled, **or** a sprig of thyme, optional*
*1 – 2 tbsps butter **or***
1 – 2 tbsps olive oil
salt and freshly ground black pepper
*pinch of cayenne pepper **or***
pinch of chili powder, optional

PREPARATION

1 Cut the pepper into even-sized chunks and place in a saucepan with the stock or water and the garlic or thyme if using. Bring to a boil, reduce the heat, cover, and simmer until the pepper is tender: about 10 minutes. Remove the garlic or thyme, if used.
2 Pour the pepper and stock or water into a food processor or blender, and purée.
3 Add the butter or oil and blend again.
4 Pass the sauce through a strainer back into the pan (to serve warm) or into a bowl (to serve chilled), and season with salt, black pepper, and, if you like, cayenne pepper or chili powder.
5 Reheat gently and serve warm, or serve chilled from the refrigerator. The sauce can be transferred to a sauceboat, or, if preferred, spooned around individual portions on the plates.

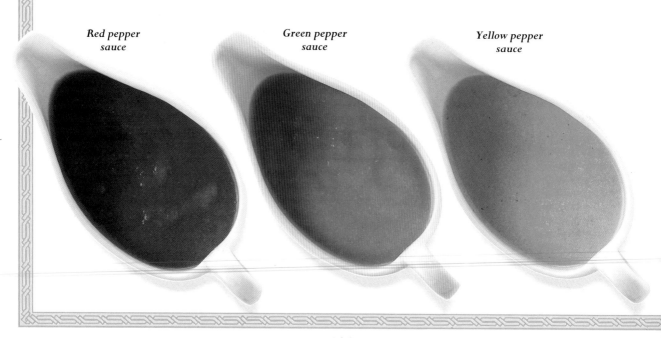

Red pepper sauce

Green pepper sauce

Yellow pepper sauce

Fresh Tomato Sauce

You need a food processor or blender to make this sauce, but it couldn't be easier. Makes 1¼ cups.

INGREDIENTS

1 tbsp olive oil
1 small onion, finely chopped
1 chopped clove garlic, optional
8 medium fresh tomatoes, quartered
salt

PREPARATION

1 Warm the oil in a large saucepan over moderate heat, add the onion, and garlic, if desired, cover, and cook until tender: about 4 minutes.
2 Add the tomatoes, and reduce the heat. Cover, and cook until the tomatoes have collapsed: about 15 minutes. Take off the heat, and leave to cool.
3 Pour the tomatoes into a food processor or blender, and purée. Pass through a strainer back into the pan, and season with salt. Gently reheat just before serving, or serve cold.

Sundried Tomato Sauce

A rich and flavorful sauce, for which you need a food processor or blender. Makes 1¼ cups.

INGREDIENTS

2 tbsps oil from the sundried tomatoes
or olive oil
1 small onion, finely chopped
1 chopped clove garlic, optional
14oz can whole peeled tomatoes,
coarsely chopped, with juice
4 sundried tomatoes in oil
2 tsps balsamic vinegar
salt and freshly ground black pepper

PREPARATION

1 Warm the oil in a large saucepan over moderate heat, add the onion, and garlic, if using, cover, and cook until tender: about 4 minutes.
2 Add the tomatoes, and reduce the heat. Cook, uncovered, until any excess liquid has evaporated and the mixture looks thick: about 15 minutes. Take off the heat and leave to cool.
3 Add the sundried tomatoes, pour the mixture into a food processor or blender, and purée. Pass through a strainer back into the pan, and add the vinegar. Season to taste and gently reheat before serving, or serve cold.

Basic Tomato Sauce

If you have no fresh tomatoes, or you like a strongly flavored tomato sauce, try this one. It is ideal for pasta, pizzas, lasagna, and other dishes requiring tomato sauce, and is also good as an accompaniment. Makes 1¼ cups.

INGREDIENTS

1 tbsp olive oil
1 small onion, finely chopped
1 chopped clove garlic, optional
14oz can whole peeled tomatoes, with juice
salt

PREPARATION

1 Warm the oil in a saucepan over moderate heat, add the onion, and garlic, if desired, cover, and cook until tender: about 4 minutes.
2 Add the tomatoes, and reduce the heat. Cook, uncovered, until any excess liquid has evaporated and the mixture looks thick: about 15 minutes. Take off the heat and leave to cool.
3 Pour the tomatoes into a food processor or blender, and purée. Pass through a strainer back into the pan and season with salt. Gently reheat just before serving, or serve cold.

Red Wine Sauce

A delicious, festive sauce. Makes 1¼ cups.

INGREDIENTS

¼ cup butter
2 shallots, finely chopped
2 tsps finely chopped fresh thyme
1 chopped clove garlic, optional
1¼ cups red wine
3 tbsps port or other fortified wine
1 vegetable stock cube
salt and freshly ground black pepper

PREPARATION

1 Melt half the butter in a medium-sized pan over moderate heat, and put the rest of the butter in the refrigerator.
2 Add the shallots, and thyme, and garlic, if using, to the pan, cover, and cook for 5 minutes. Add the wine, port, and stock cube, season well, and bring to a boil. Cook until reduced by half.
3 Cut the butter into small pieces and, just before serving, take the sauce off the heat and whisk in the butter, a little at a time, to make it glossy.

MAYONNAISE

A food processor or blender makes mayonnaise easy to prepare. The handmade version, below, needs more work but is equally successful. Makes 1 cup.

INGREDIENTS

2 large egg yolks
¼ tsp mustard powder
¼ tsp salt
2–3 grindings of black pepper
2 tsps white wine vinegar
2 tsps lemon juice
1 cup peanut or light olive oil

PREPARATION

1 Put all the ingredients except the oil into a food processor or blender. Blend at medium speed for 1 minute until everything is well mixed.
2 Turn the speed up to high and start to add the oil, drop by drop, through the top of the machine.

When you have added about half, the sound made by the sauce in the blender will change to a "glug-glug." At this point start adding the oil more quickly, pouring it in a thin stream.
3 Taste the sauce and adjust the seasoning if necessary. If the mayonnaise seems too thick, thin it by beating in a teaspoon or two of boiling water. Serve cold. Mayonnaise keeps for up to 5 days, tightly covered, in the refrigerator.

VARIATIONS

HERBED MAYONNAISE Stir 2 – 4 tablespoons of finely chopped fresh herbs into the mayonnaise. Use a mixture of herbs if desired, such as parsley and chives, with a third chosen from cilantro, basil, tarragon, or mint. Cilantro mayonnaise, for example, suits grain and legume dishes, while tarragon mayonnaise makes a salad very special.
GARLIC MAYONNAISE (AÏOLI) Crush 1 – 4 cloves of garlic and add to the blender with the other ingredients in step 1.

MAKING MAYONNAISE BY HAND

1 Whisk together all the ingredients except the oil. Add half the oil, drop by drop, whisking all the time. A dish cloth will prevent the bowl from sliding over the worktop as you whisk.

2 The sauce begins to thicken once about half the oil has been added. At this stage, add the oil faster, pouring it in a thin stream while you continue to whisk vigorously.

3 The finished mayonnaise is rich and thick (if the sauce curdles, the oil was added too quickly. Put an egg yolk in a separate bowl and gradually whisk the curdled mixture into this).

Stir finely chopped parsley and chives into mayonnaise to create a versatile herbed version. The further addition of basil gives the mayonnaise a particular affinity for tomato-based dishes.

Chives

Parsley

Basil

HOLLANDAISE SAUCE

Like mayonnaise, this is an extremely rich, thickened sauce, but it is served warm rather than cold, and most of its richness comes from butter rather than oil. Serve with steamed asparagus, broccoli, leeks, or whole artichokes for a special treat. Makes 1 cup.

INGREDIENTS

2 tbsps white wine vinegar
1 cup butter
2 large egg yolks
salt and freshly ground black pepper

PREPARATION

1 Put the wine vinegar in a small pan with 3 tablespoons of water, bring to a boil, and reduce down to a tablespoon of liquid. Allow to cool.
2 Put the butter into another small pan and heat until foaming.
3 Place the egg yolks and the reduced vinegar in a food processor or blender and blend until combined well.
4 With the motor running, slowly pour in the butter. As the mixture thickens, add the butter more quickly. Season with salt and pepper. Serve at once, or keep warm for a few hours in a thermos or in a bowl over a pan of steaming water.
HANDMADE HOLLANDAISE Reduce the vinegar and water as described in step 1, above. Set a bowl over a pan of gently steaming water on low heat. Put the egg yolks, reduced vinegar, salt, and black pepper into the bowl and whisk until thick and pale: 3 – 5 minutes. Cut the slightly softened butter into ¼-inch cubes and whisk into the egg yolk mixture a piece at a time. The sauce thickens as the butter is added. Serve the sauce at once or keep it warm in the bowl over the pan of steaming water.

VARIATIONS

MALTAISE SAUCE This is hollandaise flavored with the grated zest and the juice of an orange, preferably a blood orange; it is the classic sauce for asparagus. Intensify the flavor of the juice by reducing it to 2 tablespoons, then add 1 tablespoon of grated zest. Use in place of the vinegar.
HERBED HOLLANDAISE Stir 2 tablespoons of mixed, chopped fresh herbs into the sauce before serving; parsley, tarragon, and chervil make a good combination. Serve with steamed vegetables or a roulade such as Cashew with Broccoli (page 96).
HOLLANDAISE WITH MUSTARD For a strongly flavored, tangy sauce, add a teaspoon or so of Dijon mustard to the egg yolks at step 3.

BASIL PESTO SAUCE

Homemade pesto is much fresher and more fragrant than the store-bought variety. Thin with a little warm water for a more pourable sauce. Store, covered, in the refrigerator for up to 5 days. Makes ⅔ cup.

INGREDIENTS

1 clove garlic
¼ cup pinenuts or cashews
6 tbsps finely chopped basil leaves
⅓ cup freshly grated Parmesan cheese
5 tbsps olive oil
salt and freshly ground black pepper

PREPARATION

Blend the ingredients into a thick green cream using a food processor or blender.
HANDMADE PESTO Crush the garlic using a pestle and mortar. Add the pinenuts or cashews, and crush them to a paste. Add the basil and Parmesan, pound them well, then gradually stir in the olive oil to make a thick green cream.

QUICK HERB SAUCE

This is a quick, fresh-tasting sauce. Makes 1 cup.

INGREDIENTS

4 tbsps finely chopped fresh herbs, such as chives or flat-leaf parsley
1 cup crème fraîche or thick yogurt
salt and freshly ground black pepper

PREPARATION

Stir the herbs into the crème fraîche or yogurt, and season to taste. Serve at once, or chill in the refrigerator, and serve later the same day.

AVOCADO SAUCE

Delicately flavored yet rich, this sauce is excellent with bean and grain dishes. Makes about 1 cup.

INGREDIENTS

1 large ripe avocado, halved, pit removed
1 – 2 tbsps lemon juice, freshly squeezed
salt and freshly ground black pepper

PREPARATION

Spoon the avocado flesh from the skin into a small bowl. Add the lemon juice, season with salt and black pepper, and mash well with a fork. Serve the sauce at once: it does not keep.

DESSERTS

Presenting your guests with a fabulous dessert is the way to round off any meal with a flourish. This irresistible selection includes creamy chocolate creations and unusual sorbets, traditional pies, as well as light, fruit-based desserts and perfect homemade ice creams.

VANILLA-POACHED PEARS

Choose even-sized, firm pears for this recipe. Poached pears can be served as they are, or with Vanilla Ice Cream (right) or chocolate sauce (below). Serves 4.

INGREDIENTS

¾ cup superfine sugar
zest of ½ lemon, pared in one long strip
1 vanilla bean, split lengthways
1¼ cups water
4 pears, peeled, with stalks intact

PREPARATION

1 Pour the sugar into a saucepan large enough for the pears, and add the lemon zest, vanilla bean, and water. Dissolve the sugar over moderate heat.
2 Put the pears into the liquid, bring the mixture to a gentle simmer, then reduce the heat, cover, and leave to cook until the pears are tender right through when pierced with a sharp knife or skewer: 20–30 minutes. Remove from the pan using a slotted spoon and place in a serving dish.
3 Turn up the heat, and let the liquid boil until it has reduced a little to make a syrup: about 5 minutes. Discard the zest, and pour the syrup, together with the vanilla bean, over the pears. Allow to cool, then refrigerate before serving.

CHOCOLATE SAUCE

INGREDIENTS

8oz semi-sweet chocolate, broken into pieces
¼ cup butter
¼ cup water

PREPARATION

1 Place the ingredients in a bowl and set over a saucepan of gently simmering water. Leave until the contents have melted, stirring occasionally.
2 Remove the bowl from the saucepan and beat the contents until smooth and creamy. Serve warm.

VANILLA ICE CREAM

Vanilla sugar enhances the flavor of this ice cream. To make it, break a vanilla bean in half, and bury the halves in sugar. As you use the sugar, replace with more. This ice cream is best eaten within 48 hours. Serves 4.

INGREDIENTS

1¼ cups light cream
1 vanilla bean
4 egg yolks
⅓ cup sugar, preferably flavored with a vanilla bean (see note above)
½ tsp vanilla extract
1¼ cups heavy cream

PREPARATION

1 Put the light cream into a saucepan with the vanilla bean, and bring to a boil. Remove from the heat, cover, and set aside: this allows the cream to absorb the flavor of the vanilla.
2 Whisk the egg yolks and sugar in a bowl until creamy and pale: 2–3 minutes.
3 Reheat the cream to the boiling point, then pour it through a strainer onto the egg yolks and sugar, and stir well to combine (rinse the vanilla bean and dry it; it can be reused many times).
4 Pour the mixture back into the saucepan, and stir it over low heat until it just thickens and thinly coats the back of a spoon: 2–3 minutes. Be sure to heat it gently to avoid curdling. Stir in the vanilla extract, and set the mixture aside to cool.
5 Whip the heavy cream until it forms soft peaks and fold into the vanilla mixture. Pour into a shallow metal pan. Freeze until it begins to solidify around the edges: 15–30 minutes.
6 Take out the partially frozen mixture, and whisk it well. Return to the freezer for 15–30 minutes, then whisk again. Repeat until the ice cream is too thick to whisk, then leave it to freeze completely.
7 Around 20 minutes before serving, take the ice cream out of the freezer, and allow it to soften at room temperature. Serve in scoops.

CHOCOLATE & GINGER ROULADE

Rich, creamy, and utterly delicious, this is a real treat. Serves 6.

INGREDIENTS

6 large eggs, separated
⅔ cup superfine sugar
½ cup cocoa powder
powdered sugar, for dusting
THE FILLING
1¼ cups cream
¼ cup syrup from the ginger (see below)
4 pieces preserved stem ginger in syrup, finely chopped

PREPARATION

1 Preheat the oven to 375°F/190°C. Line a
9 x 13-inch jelly roll pan with waxed paper.
2 Whisk the egg whites in a clean bowl until stiff.
3 In another large bowl, whisk the egg yolks with the superfine sugar until thick and fluffy. Using a metal spoon, fold in the cocoa powder, then gently fold in the egg whites.
4 Pour the mixture into the prepared pan, smoothing it to the edges. Bake until risen and just firm in the center: about 15 minutes. Leave the roulade base to cool in the pan; it will shrink a great deal. Then remove from the pan, face down, onto a piece of waxed paper dusted with powdered sugar. Peel the waxed paper from the top.
5 Prepare the filling. Whip the cream until it forms soft peaks, then whip in the ginger syrup. Stir in the chopped ginger. Spread the cream over the roulade, leaving a ½-inch border all around (to make rolling up easier).
6 Roll up the roulade (see page 95 for the technique). Wrap it in waxed paper and chill for at least 30 minutes before slicing it. Serve with warm chocolate sauce (facing page).

DOUBLE-CHOCOLATE BROWNIES WITH HAZELNUTS

These are a chocoholic's delight: they are made from baker's chocolate and packed with white chocolate, along with toasted hazelnuts. Serve them warm, as a dessert, with crème fraîche or thick yogurt, or allow them to cool, and serve with coffee. Makes 12.

INGREDIENTS

5oz semi-sweet chocolate, broken into pieces
¼ cup butter
2 eggs
¼ cup brown sugar
2oz white chocolate, cut into small pieces
⅓ cup hazelnuts, toasted briefly under a preheated broiler and roughly chopped

PREPARATION

1 Preheat the oven to 350°F/180°C. Line a
8-inch square baking pan with waxed paper.
2 Put the chocolate and butter into a bowl, and set over a saucepan of gently simmering water. Leave until melted, stirring occasionally to combine the ingredients.
3 Meanwhile, break the eggs into a large bowl, and add the sugar. Beat the eggs and sugar until they are thick and pale and the trail that the beaters leave in the mixture remains visible for several seconds. This is very quickly done using an electric beater at top speed; with a hand whisk it takes around 10 minutes.
4 Pour the melted chocolate and butter mixture on top of the whisked egg mixture, and fold it in with a metal spoon, then gently fold in the white chocolate and nuts.
5 Pour this mixture into the pan, then bake in the oven until slightly risen and crusty looking:
25 minutes (a skewer inserted into the center will not come out clean because the brownies will be moist and slightly runny inside).

LAVENDER HONEY ICE CREAM

Lavender flowers give this ice cream an unusual, almost peppery flavor that I find very enjoyable in contrast with the honey. Intensely flavored Provençal lavender honey can be used instead of clear honey and lavender flowers; in this case, omit step 1. Serves 4.

INGREDIENTS

1¼ cups light cream
6 heads of lavender flowers, plus extra to garnish
4 egg yolks
3 tbsps superfine sugar
2 tbsps clear honey
1¼ cups heavy cream

PREPARATION

1 Put the light cream into a saucepan with the 6 lavender flowers and bring to a boil. Remove from the heat, cover, and set aside: this allows the cream to absorb the flavor of the lavender flowers.
2 Whisk the egg yolks and sugar in a bowl until creamy and pale: 2–3 minutes.
3 Reheat the cream to the boiling point, then pour it through a strainer onto the egg yolks and sugar, and stir well to combine.
4 Pour the mixture back into the saucepan, and stir it over low heat until it just thickens and thinly coats the back of a spoon: 2–3 minutes. Be sure to heat it gently to avoid it curdling. Stir in the honey, and set the mixture aside to cool.
5 Whip the heavy cream until it forms soft peaks and fold into the lavender mixture. Pour into a shallow metal pan. Freeze until it begins to solidify around the edges: 15–30 minutes.
6 Take out the partially frozen mixture, and whisk it well. Return to the freezer for 15–30 minutes, then whisk again. Repeat until the ice cream is too thick to whisk, then leave it to freeze completely.
7 About 20 minutes before serving, take the ice cream out of the freezer, and allow it to soften at room temperature. Serve it in scoops, decorated with lavender flowers.

AMARETTO PARFAIT WITH RASPBERRY COULIS

A parfait is a very rich ice cream that does not need stirring during the freezing process and is soft enough to serve straight from the freezer. You need an electric beater to make this recipe. Serves 4 to 6.

INGREDIENTS

6 egg yolks
⅔ cup superfine sugar
¼ cup amaretto liqueur
1 cup flaked almonds, toasted and cooled
2½ cups heavy cream
THE COULIS
1 lb fresh or frozen raspberries
2 tbsps superfine sugar
2 tbsps water

PREPARATION

1 Put the egg yolks into a large bowl and whisk until thick and pale.
2 Put the sugar into a small saucepan with 4 tablespoons of water and heat gently until the sugar has melted. Then raise the heat and let the syrup boil until a drop is thick enough to form a thread when pulled: 1–2 minutes. Be sure not to go past this stage or the syrup will become too hard.
3 Pour the syrup onto the egg yolks, whisking all the time. Continue to whisk until the mixture is very thick and has cooled a little: about 5 minutes.
4 Stir in the amaretto and most of the almonds (reserving a few for decoration). Whip the cream until it forms soft peaks and fold that in, too.
5 Turn the parfait into a 2-pint mold, loaf pan, or other suitable container and freeze until solid.
6 While the parfait is freezing, make the coulis. Put the raspberries into a blender and purée, then strain them into a saucepan. Alternatively, press them through a strainer directly into the saucepan. Add the sugar and water, place over moderate heat, and bring to a boil. Boil for 1 minute (this makes the coulis clear and glossy). Remove from the heat and allow to cool.
7 To serve the parfait, loosen the sides, and turn it out onto a plate, or serve it from the container in scoops. Pour a little of the raspberry coulis over and around each serving, and scatter with the reserved almonds.

ROSE SORBET

*One of my favorite desserts, this fragrant pink sorbet
is best made from the deepest red, most heavily
perfumed roses you can find, but I have also made it
successfully from less than perfect roses.
Illustrated on page 129. Serves 4.*

INGREDIENTS

*petals from 4 large, fragrant, red roses
1 cup superfine sugar
1¼ cups water
1 lemon
rose petals to decorate*

PREPARATION

1 Put the rose petals, sugar, and water into a
saucepan and heat gently so that the sugar dissolves
by the time the mixture boils. Boil for 5 minutes,
then remove from the heat, and leave to cool.
2 Strain the rose petal mixture through a strainer
into a bowl. Squeeze the lemon, and add its juice
to the mixture in the bowl.
3 Transfer the sorbet mixture to a plastic
container and freeze, uncovered, stirring often to
help break up the crystals of ice. Alternatively,
freeze until solid without stirring – for about 6
hours or overnight – then cut it into small chunks
and put in a food processor or blender. Blend for a
minute or two until the sorbet is soft and fluffy,
then return it to the container and freeze again.
4 Serve in scoops, straight from the freezer, and
decorated with reserved rose petals.

PASSION FRUIT & LIME SORBET

*This sorbet is easy to make and has a wonderful flavor.
I like it with the seeds of the passion fruit left in because
they give the sorbet a crunchy texture and a pretty,
speckled appearance, but you can strain the mixture
to remove them, if preferred. Serves 4.*

INGREDIENTS

*1 cup superfine sugar
1¼ cups water
12 passion fruit, halved
1 lime*

PREPARATION

1 Dissolve the sugar in the water in a saucepan
over low heat, then raise the heat, bring to a boil,
and cook until the mixture thickens to a syrup:
3–4 minutes. Remove from the heat and set aside
to cool completely.

2 Scoop the pulp and seeds from the passion fruit
and add to the syrup, pressing them through a nylon
strainer first to remove the seeds, if preferred.
3 Pare long, thin shreds of zest from the lime, and
add most of them to the sorbet mixture, reserving
some for decoration. Wrap the reserved shreds in
plastic wrap to prevent them from drying out.
Squeeze the lime, and add the juice to the mixture.
4 Transfer the sorbet mixture to a plastic
container and freeze, uncovered, stirring often to
help break up the crystals of ice. Alternatively,
freeze until solid without stirring – for about 6
hours or overnight – then cut it into small chunks
and put in a food processor or blender. Blend for a
minute or two until the sorbet is soft and fluffy,
then return to the container and freeze again.
5 Serve in scoops, straight from the freezer,
decorated with shreds of lime zest.

TROPICAL FRUIT SALAD

*One of the prettiest and healthiest desserts of all, this
can be made from any colorful, exotic fruits that are
available. The fruit should be ripe. You may need to buy
it a day or two in advance to allow time for it to ripen.
Serve the salad with Rose Sorbet or Passion Fruit and
Lime Sorbet (this page), thick yogurt, crème fraîche, or
simply on its own. Illustrated on page 128. Serves 6.*

INGREDIENTS

*4–6 ripe figs
2 starfruit (carambola)
1 wedge of watermelon
1 large mango
1 small papaya
1 pomegranate*

PREPARATION

1 Cut each fig into eight segments. Thinly slice
the starfruit. Peel the wedge of watermelon, and
cut the flesh into long, thin slices.
2 Make two cuts down the length of the mango,
each about ¼-inch from the stem, going right
through the fruit so that the two halves fall away
(leaving a middle section that consists of the large
flat pit). Remove the skin from the two halves, and
cut the flesh into long, thin slices.
3 Cut the papaya in half, scoop out the shiny black
seeds, remove the peel, and cut the flesh into
long, thin slices.
4 Halve the pomegranate, and scoop out the
seeds, removing any fibrous membrane.
5 Arrange the fruit on a plate, and scatter the
pomegranate seeds over the top. Serve at once.

Tropical fruit salad
(page 127)

*Rose sorbet
(page 127)*

*Strawberry pavlova
(page 130)*

STRAWBERRY PAVLOVAS

The meringue for these pavlovas is baked at a very low temperature to give it a lovely marshmallowy center with a crisp outside. Although pavlova is often made as one large meringue, individual portions are also successful; this recipe makes six. Other pretty, soft fruit may be used instead of the strawberries. Illustrated on pages 128–9. Serves 6.

INGREDIENTS

3 egg whites
¾ cup sugar
1 tsp vanilla extract
1 tsp cornstarch
1 tsp white wine vinegar
1¼ cups heavy cream
½–¾lb small, ripe strawberries, hulled (leaves reserved for garnish)

PREPARATION

1 Preheat the oven to 250°F/130°C. Line a large baking sheet with waxed paper.
2 Whisk the egg whites in a large, clean bowl until stiff.
3 Add the sugar to the egg whites, a heaped tablespoon at a time, whisking well after each addition so the meringue is stiff and glossy.
4 Add the vanilla extract, cornstarch, and vinegar, and fold in with a large metal spoon.
5 Spoon the meringue into six mounds on the baking sheet, leaving space around each one. Spread each mound into a circle, making the center flat and fluffing up the sides with a palette knife.
6 Bake until dry and crisp on the outside and still slightly soft in the center: 1–1½ hours. Leave to cool, then peel them off the paper.

The meringues will keep, in foil or in an airtight container, for up to 1 week in a dry place.

7 Place the meringues on individual plates or in a serving dish. Whip the cream until thick and spoon a little into the center of each pavlova.
8 Halve most of the strawberries, and arrange them over the cream. Decorate the plate with leaves and whole strawberries. Serve at once, or store in the refrigerator for up to two hours.

STRAWBERRY CHEESECAKE

A party piece, this luscious cheesecake has a delectable strawberry topping. It is best made a day ahead, with the topping, which can be varied according to the fruit in season, added later. Serves 8.

INGREDIENTS

1½ cups graham crackers
3 tbsps butter
3 tbsps granulated sugar
2 cups ricotta cheese
¾ cup superfine sugar
⅔ cup heavy cream
3 eggs, separated
juice and finely grated zest of 1 lemon
1 tsp vanilla extract
1lb small, ripe strawberries, hulled
1 cup red currant jelly

PREPARATION

1 Preheat the oven to 300°F/150°C. Line the base and sides of an 8-inch springform pan with waxed paper.
2 On the work counter, run a rolling pin over the crackers to crush them. Melt the butter in a small saucepan, add the crumbled crackers and the sugar, stir well to combine and spoon into the prepared pan. Press down firmly using the back of a spoon. Set aside while you prepare the cheesecake mixture.
3 Put the ricotta cheese into a large bowl, break it up with a fork, then add the superfine sugar, cream, egg yolks, lemon juice and zest, and vanilla extract. Beat until the consistency is smooth.
4 Whisk the egg whites in another clean bowl until they are stiff, gently fold into the cheesecake mixture using a metal spoon. Pour over the crust in the pan.
5 Bake until the cheesecake is set and a skewer inserted into the center comes out clean: about 1½ hours. Turn the oven off but leave the cake inside to cool down gently (don't worry about cracks in the cake; most of these disappear as the cake cools further and shrinks).
6 Remove the cheesecake from the oven after an hour or so, cool completely, then chill in the refrigerator for about 2–3 hours.
7 Arrange the strawberries on top. If they are small they can be used whole, with their points up and their stem ends trimmed so they stand level; if large, cut them in half. Melt the red currant jelly in a saucepan and spoon over the strawberries to make a thick shiny glaze. Leave until the jelly has cooled and set, then serve.

BLUEBERRY PIE

This double-crust pie can be made with different fruit or with mixtures of fruit. Serve it with Vanilla Ice Cream (page 124), thick yogurt, or crème fraîche. Serves 4.

INGREDIENTS

RICH CRUST PASTRY

2½ cups all-purpose flour
¾ cup butter, cut into small pieces
¼ cup powdered sugar
1 egg yolk

THE FILLING

1½lb blueberries
½ cup superfine sugar
2 tbsps cornstarch
1 tbsp lemon juice
milk, to glaze
superfine sugar, to sprinkle

PREPARATION

1 Preheat the oven to 375°F/190°C.

2 Sift the flour into a large bowl or the bowl of a food processor, and add the butter, powdered sugar, and egg yolk. Rub the ingredients together with your fingertips, or work briefly in the food processor until a dough has just formed.

3 Turn the dough out onto a lightly floured surface and divide into two pieces, one slightly larger than the other, and knead each one into a smooth round. Wrap in plastic wrap and chill in the refrigerator for a few minutes.

4 Place the blueberries, sugar, cornstarch, and lemon juice in a bowl and mix to combine well.

5 Roll out the smaller piece of pastry on a floured board to fit a 10-inch pie plate or shallow quiche dish. Line the plate or dish with the pastry. Pile the blueberry mixture into the dish, leaving a clear ½-inch border all round if you are using a pie plate. Brush the edges with cold water.

6 Roll out the rest of the pastry and place over the fruit. Press the pastry edges together and trim. Flute and scallop the pie rim as shown on page 151. Use a skewer to make two or three steam holes in the center, then decorate the pie with pastry trimmings.

7 Brush the pie with a little milk, sprinkle with superfine sugar, and bake until golden brown: 30 minutes. Serve warm.

LEMON TART

Crisp pastry contrasts with cool, tangy lemon to make a refreshing dessert. I like it just as it is, although you could serve cream or crème fraîche with it. Serves 4.

INGREDIENTS

CRUST PASTRY

1 cup all-purpose flour
5 tbsps butter, cut into small pieces

THE FILLING

2 large lemons
⅔ cup superfine sugar
2 eggs
⅔ cup heavy cream
lemon strips (page 145) to decorate, optional

PREPARATION

1 Preheat the oven to 400°F/200°C.

2 Sift the flour into a large bowl or the bowl of a food processor, and add the butter. Rub the butter into the flour with your fingertips, or work briefly in the food processor until a dough has just formed. Add a little cold water – perhaps a teaspoonful – to make the dough hold together.

3 Turn the dough out onto a lightly floured surface and roll to fit a 8-inch shallow, loose-bottomed quiche pan. Slide the pastry off the board and onto the pan. Press it in place, trim it (reserve trimmings), and prick the base (see page 151).

4 Bake the tart shell until it is crisp, firm to the touch, and turning golden brown: about 15 minutes. Remove and set aside. Turn the oven setting down to 250°F/130°C.

5 Make the lemon filling. Finely grate the zest of the lemons into a bowl. Squeeze the lemon juice and add to the bowl. Add the sugar and eggs and whisk to combine. Pour in the cream and whisk again until the consistency is smooth.

6 Fill in any cracks in the pastry shell with pastry trimmings, then pour in the lemon mixture and bake the tart in the oven until the filling has set and feels firm to a light touch in the middle: about 40 minutes.

7 Take the tart out of the oven and allow it to cool, then chill it in the refrigerator to firm up the lemon custard. Remove it from the pan, place on a serving plate and decorate, if desired, sprinkling lemon strips over the top. Serve chilled.

JEWELED FRUIT TART

*Use any colorful fruits you like for this tart, but make
sure they are completely ripe. This recipe makes one
large tart or four individual ones. Serves 4.*

INGREDIENTS

*butter to grease the baking sheet
½lb homemade quick flaky pastry
(page 150) or frozen puff pastry
1 egg, beaten
6 tbsps apricot jam
1 tbsp lemon juice
1 cup blueberries
12 strawberries, hulled
2 kiwi, peeled, halved lengthways,
and thickly sliced
3 ripe figs, quartered
1 cup red currants
8 cape gooseberries, papery sepals pulled back **or**
cherries, leaves and stems attached*

PREPARATION

1 Preheat the oven to 425°F/220°C. Lightly
grease a baking sheet with butter.
2 Roll out the pastry on a floured board and cut
out one 10 x 10-inch square or four 5 x 5-inch
squares. Place the square(s) on the baking sheet,
and brush the edges with water.
3 Cut the remaining pastry into long, thin strips
about ¾-inch wide and place them around the
edges to make a single-layer border. Decorate the
border by pressing the back of a knife into it in a
pattern, then "flake" the sides by cutting into them
horizontally, again with the back of a knife, to
encourage the pastry to rise in flakes. Brush the
top of the border with the beaten egg, being
careful not to get any egg on the sides.
4 Bake the pastry shell(s) until golden brown and
risen: about 20 minutes. Remove from the oven
and leave on a wire rack to cool.
5 Put the jam into a small saucepan with the
lemon juice and melt over gentle heat, then
transfer to a small bowl, straining to remove any
lumps of apricot. Brush a little of this glaze over
the base of the pastry shell(s).
6 Arrange the fruit in the pastry shell, piled
generously high. Place strawberries with the pointed
ends upward and any cut fruit with the cut side
down. Follow the pattern here, or create your own
design with diagonal or straight lines. Alternatively,
make the fruit radiate out from the center.
7 Reheat the remaining glaze and spoon it over
the fruit to cover it thickly. Allow the glaze to
cool and gel, then serve.

Blueberries

*Lemon
juice*

Apricot jam

Beaten egg

Flaky pastry

Kiwi fruit

Figs

Red currants

Strawberries

Cape gooseberries

MENU PLANNING

Menu planning really begins in the store or market, where you can buy the fresh ingredients and then plan a menu around them. Balance rich dishes with simple ones, making sure that colors and textures are varied, and try not to repeat a key ingredient. If possible, use serving dishes that complement the food. Most of all, a menu *you* like is one your guests are most likely to enjoy.

BRUNCHES & LIGHT LUNCHES

These are easy, informal menus, suitable for lunch or brunch.
A fruit juice, or even mimosa, makes a good apéritif, and you
could also serve a fruit salad as a refreshing first course.
Mix and match between the menus to cook for a large group
of people or to introduce more variety.

BRUNCH PARTY

Warm Pasta Salad with Tomato and Basil **or**
*Warm Pasta Salad with Grilled Pepper and
Arugula (page 56)*

•

Vegetable Frittata (page 98) **or**
Four-cheese Soufflé (page 26)

Mixed Leaf Salad with Flowers and Herbs (page 52)

Light Bread Rolls (page 103), served warm

•

Blueberry Pie (page 131)

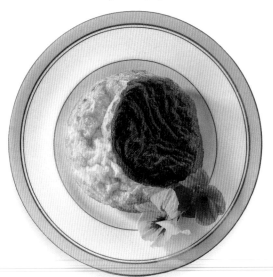

Four-cheese soufflé

LUNCH PARTY

*Twice-baked Mushroom or Goat Cheese and
Thyme Soufflés (page 93)*

•

Vegetable Paella (page 113) **or**
Porcini Risotto (page 114)

*Endive, Watercress, Fennel, Red Onion,
and Orange Salad (page 48)*

•

Strawberry Cheesecake (page 130)

Vegetable paella

INFORMAL SUPPER PARTIES

It's fun to plan an informal supper around a theme, as I've done here. Other possible themes are fondue, which makes a good main dish for 2 to 6 people, or pizza, which can be served do-it-yourself style with lots of toppings to choose from. To feed a crowd, you may want to serve several main courses together: when cooking pasta, this means using several large saucepans at once and preparing the sauces ahead of time.

PASTA SUPPER

Vegetables à la Grecque (page 60) **or**
Insalata Tricolore (page 51)

•

Farfalle with Broccoli Cream Sauce (page 88) **or**
*Rigatoni with Tomato, Eggplant, and
Red Peppers (page 91)*

Arugula Salad with Flakes of Parmesan (page 53)

•

Selection of Ice Creams (pages 124 and 126) **or**
Fresh Fruit

INDIAN SUPPER

Spiced Vegetable Triangles (page 110) **or**
*Mustard Seed Crêpes with Spiced Vegetable
Filling (page 79)*

•

Cashew Korma (page 70)

Bombay Potatoes (page 86)

Spiced Okra (page 86) **or**
Green Beans with Cumin (page 83)

Spinach Dal (page 117)

Spiced Rice (page 115)

•

Rose Sorbet (page 127) **or**
Tropical Fruit Salad (page 127)

Rigatoni with tomato, eggplant, and red peppers

Cashew korma

SIMPLE MEALS

The first supper is based on a choice of stir-fries. These versatile and satisfying dishes can be put together in a few minutes and the meal can be finished off with fresh fruit, yogurt, or ice cream. The second supper requires advance preparation and slow cooking, but is perfect for feeding a crowd, especially when you don't know exactly what time everyone is going to arrive.

QUICK SUPPER

Thai-style Stir-fry Vegetables (page 32)
with Boiled Rice **or**
Summer Stir-fry with Toasted Almonds (page 72)
with Boiled Rice

•

Fresh Fruit, Yogurt, or Cheese and Crackers

PREPARE-AHEAD SUPPER

Potato and Leek Soup (page 46)

Garlic or Herb Bread (page 47)

•

Spinach, Tomato, and Mozzarella Lasagna (page 89)

Mixed Salad Leaves

•

Jeweled Fruit Tart (page 132)

Jeweled fruit tart

QUICK & EASY IDEAS

These ideas are for quick everyday meals when you have very little time; I've included a list of straightforward one-course meals and undemanding accompaniments with the assumption that you'll serve a simple dessert such as fresh seasonal fruit or tasty cheese. Dress salad leaves in 3 parts olive oil to 1 part balsamic vinegar, with salt and freshly ground black pepper added to taste.

Fresh herb omelette

—— 1 ——

Fresh Herb Omelette (page 14)

Mixed Salad Leaves

—— 2 ——

Insalata Tricolore (page 51)

Warm Pasta Salad (chosen from page 56)

—— 3 ——

Deep-fried Brie with Apricot Sauce (page 97)

Mixed Salad Leaves

Crusty Bread

—— 4 ——

Oak Leaf Lettuce, Avocado, and Roasted Cashews (page 50)

Crusty Bread

Assorted Cheeses

—— 5 ——

Vegetarian Salade Niçoise (page 53)

Baguette

—— 6 ——

Roasted Root Vegetables (page 75)

Quick Herb Sauce (page 123)

Crusty Bread

—— 7 ——

Spinach Dal (page 117)

Sliced Tomatoes and Onions

Poppadums and Mango Chutney

—— 8 ——

Roasted Mediterranean Vegetables (page 75)

Olives

Ciabatta Bread

Mixed Salad Leaves

—— 9 ——

Vegetable Frittata (page 98)

Fresh Watercress

Vegetable frittata

PARTIES

The recipe suggestions are for two different kinds of parties: a cocktail party where you serve finger food along with the liquid refreshments; and a buffet party where guests help themselves to more substantial food. In both cases, color and contrast of dishes are important. To determine quantities, start from first principles: decide how many slices or portions one guest might have, then multiply by the number of guests.

COCKTAIL PARTY

Goat Cheese Dip (page 58) with Crudités

Guacamole (page 59) with Crudités

•

Assorted Tiny Quiches and Tartlets (chosen from page 105)

Assorted Phyllo Parcels (chosen from pages 109–10)

Crostini with Spreads (page 47)

Baby Eggplants Stuffed with Mushrooms and Nuts (page 64)

Cream Cheese Mushrooms (page 65)

•

Tropical Fruit Salad (page 127) served in small pieces on cocktail sticks

BUFFET PARTY

A Trio of Dips: Cucumber and Mint Dip, Curried Cashew Dip, and Mushroom Dip (pages 58–9) with Melba Toast (page 47) or Crudités

•

Tomato, Zucchini, Red Pepper, and Basil Terrine (page 10)

Spinach Roulade with Cream Cheese and Peppers (page 96)

Parmigiana di Melanzane (page 74)

New Potato Salad (page 50)

Rice Salad with Herbs, Avocado, and Nuts (page 57)

Mixed Leaf Salad with Flowers and Herbs (page 52)

White Cabbage Salad (page 50)

Garlic or Herb Bread (page 47), served hot

•

Lemon Tart (page 131) **or** *Chocolate and Ginger Roulade (page 125)*

Phyllo flowers and Money bags

Spinach roulade

OUTDOOR EATING

The main constraint when packing a picnic is how well the
food will travel, but it is surprising what you can take in a
carefully packed box or picnic basket. The barbecue menu is
planned around Falafel, cooked on a flat sheet or frying
pan over the barbecue, and Mediterranean Vegetables, roasted
on the grill. Whether picnic or barbecue, provide plenty of
bread to fill up your guests and mop up your plates.

PICNIC

Leek and sesame quiche

Broccoli and Brie Quiches (page 28) *or*
Leek and Sesame Quiches (page 105)

Tabbouleh (page 57)

Peppers Filled with Grilled Vegetables (page 65)

Vegetarian Salade Niçoise (page 53)

•

Double-chocolate Brownies (page 125) *or*
Fresh Fruit

BARBECUE

Gazpacho (page 45)

•

Falafel (page 117) with Fresh or Sundried
Tomato Sauce (page 121)

Roasted Mediterranean Vegetables (page 75)

Green Leaves with Goat Cheese and Walnuts
(page 52) *or*
Arugula Salad with Flakes of Parmesan (page 53)

Potatoes or Corn Cobs, part-cooked, wrapped in foil
and buried in the fire embers

•

Blueberry Pie (page 131) *or*
Lemon Tart (page 131)

Peppers filled with grilled vegetables

Gazpacho

SPECIAL DINNERS

These are formal vegetarian meals for special events and celebrations. The meals are impressive, but not difficult. Many of the dishes, such as the roulade, can be made in advance and require only a little last-minute attention. Serving a first course that can be prepared in advance along with a simple but impressive dessert, as these menus suggest, also makes life easier. If you are nervous, have a trial run of the menu to build up confidence. Then, on the special day, relax and enjoy the party along with everyone else.

WINTER DINNER PARTY

Blue Cheese, Leek, and Watercress Terrine (page 69)
Red Wine Sauce (page 121)

•

Gruyère Gougère (page 108)

Gratin Dauphinois (page 80)

Spinach with Nutmeg (page 83)

•

Strawberry Pavlovas (page 130) **or**
Passion Fruit and Lime Sorbet (page 127)

SUMMER DINNER PARTY

Cucumber and Tarragon Soup (page 46), iced **or**
Tomato-filled Artichokes (page 22)

•

*Gruyère and Herb Roulade with Asparagus
(page 34)*

Mixed Leaf Salad with Flowers and Herbs (page 52)

Carrot and Zucchini Ribbons with Pesto (page 82)

New Potatoes

•

Strawberry Cheesecake (page 130) **or**
Rose Sorbet (page 127)

Strawberry pavlova

HOLIDAY DINNERS

Holidays are wonderful opportunities to show how delicious
vegetarian food can be. I like to serve a "showy" main course that
creates a strong focal point, such as the Cashew and Tomato Pâté
en Croûte, the Vegetable Strudel or a colorful roulade. Alongside
these dishes serve seasonal vegetables and, if you wish, traditional
trimmings such as cranberry sauce. Serve a simple but delicious
first course and a luxurious pudding at the end,
and you'll have a meal to remember.

HOLIDAY DINNER 1

*Endive, Watercress, Fennel, Red Onion,
and Orange Salad (page 48)* **or**
*Twice-baked Goat Cheese and Thyme Soufflés
(page 93)*

•

Cashew and Tomato Pâté en Croûte (page 106) **or**
Vegetable Strudel (page 16)

Red Wine Sauce (page 121)

Fantail Roast Potatoes (page 81)

Buttered Leeks with Parsley (page 83)

Celeriac Purée (page 83)

•

Chocolate and Ginger Roulade (page 125) **or**
*Vanilla-poached Pears with Ice Cream
and Chocolate Sauce (page 124)*

HOLIDAY DINNER 2

Creamy Leek and Tarragon Crêpes (page 38) **or**
Pumpkin, Broccoli, and Leek Terrine (page 69)

•

*Cheddar and Herb Roulade with
Mushrooms (page 94)*

Red Wine Sauce (page 121)

Spiced Red Cabbage and Apple (page 87)

Julienne of Kohlrabi (page 82) **or**
Roasted Root Vegetables (page 75)

•

Amaretto Parfait with Raspberry Coulis (page 126) **or**
Tropical Fruit Salad (page 127)

Cashew and tomato pâté en croûte

Creamy leek and tarragon crêpes

TECHNIQUES

*Part of the pleasure of cooking is handling
fresh fruit and vegetables, cracking eggs, choosing
herbs and spices: all part of the process of
transforming basic ingredients into delicious meals.
This section contains useful kitchen information,
such as how to prepare artichokes, make béchamel
sauce and crêpe batter, cook rice, and bake the
perfect pie crust. It also lists the essential
items for the well-stocked cupboard and
gives advice on what kitchen equipment
is indispensable.*

PREPARING VEGETABLES

A few simple techniques go a long way toward making cooking pleasurable. With garlic, for example, I pull off the papery skin and then roughly chop the flesh with a sharp knife, or crush it using the blunt side of a knife. I peel tomatoes by covering them with hot water, but I rarely seed them. The slightly indigestible skin of red peppers can be removed by roasting. The following pages show my favorite methods of preparing and cooking vegetables and – because looks are also important – the easy but effective garnishes I use.

PEELING A TOMATO

Cover the tomato with boiling water. After 10 seconds pierce the skin with the point of a knife. If the skin splits, drain the tomato and peel it; if not, leave it for a few seconds longer.

PEELING A PEPPER

Quarter the pepper. Place under a hot broiler, shiny side up, until the skin blisters and turns black. Allow to cool. Tear off the papery skin, and remove and discard the stalk and seeds.

CHOPPING FRESH HERBS

Wash fresh herbs well and dry them in a salad spinner or on paper towels. Remove large stalks from herbs such as flat-leaf parsley, then chop the herbs with a knife. Hold the point down with one hand while you rock the handle with the other, sweeping back and forth over the herbs until they are finely chopped.

GARNISHES

Garnishing a dish makes it special – and the
simpler the garnish the better. Ideally,
make creative use of ingredients from the recipe
so you have a garnish that is appropriate.

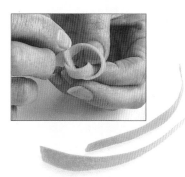

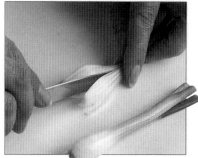

CARROT KNOT
Cut a long sliver of carrot, tie it into
a loose knot and tuck in the ends.

LEMON STRIP
Take a thin piece of zest from a lemon,
remove any pith, and cut the zest into
delicate strips, as fine as you like.

SCALLION TASSELS
Slice into one or both ends, turning the
scallion around as you cut through it.
Place in ice water so the cut ends curl.

MAKING VEGETABLE STICKS AND DICE

This is a useful and attractive way to cut many
vegetables, not just carrots. It may be easier to do
if you trim unevenly shaped vegetables first; you
can use the trimmings when making stock.

1 Cut the vegetable into parallel slices
about ¼-inch wide. If you want to
make fine strips (juliennes), cut the
slices much more thinly.

2 Stack the slices and cut down
through them to make sticks. Cut
more finely to make julienne strips.

3 Cut across the sticks to make them
into small dice, for use in soups,
sauces, and fillings.

PREPARING VEGETABLES

CHOPPING AN ONION

1 Trim the onion, removing the root, and peel off the papery skin. Wash the onion, then cut it in half from the stalk end to the root end.

2 Cut the onion along its markings from root end to tip, making the cuts close or farther apart depending on how finely chopped the onion needs to be.

3 Turn the onion and slice it again, so that the cuts are at right angles to the first ones.

SEEDING CHILIS

There are many different varieties of chili, varying greatly in hotness. They are notoriously difficult to identify, but as a general rule the smaller the chili, the hotter the flavor. If in doubt, seek advice, or better still, taste — cautiously!

1 Halve the chili, then remove the seeds, stalk, and inner white part. Be very careful not to touch your face or get juice in your eyes because chili can burn.

2 Rinse the chili under the tap. Cut lengthwise into strips, then across into small pieces. Wash your hands after handling chilis.

ARTICHOKES: PREPARING THE RAW BASE

STUFFING (COOKED)

1 Cut off the top and stalk of the uncooked artichoke, then cut away the leaves, leaving the base. Squeeze with lemon juice to preserve its color.

2 Scoop out the tiny central leaves and fluffy "choke." Rinse the base. Cook in boiling water until just tender and use as described in the recipe.

1 After boiling, press back the outer leaves, discard the central leaf cluster and scrape away the "choke." Stuff as described in the recipe.

CLEANING LEEKS

1 Cut off the root and trim the green leaves, cutting off damaged or very coarse ones.

2 Slit the leek from the top to about halfway down; rinse carefully under cold water, opening up the layers and making sure all the grit is washed away.

PREPARING GARLIC

Twist the clove of garlic between your finger and thumb to loosen the skin. Remove the skin and chop or crush the flesh using a sharp knife. To crush the flesh, press down all over it with the blunt side of a knife. For an extra smooth result, make a paste by rubbing salt into the flesh.

SALAD LEAVES

Store salad leaves unwashed in the bottom of the refrigerator, then wash thoroughly and dry before use. To dry, use a salad spinner, or drain in a colander and then dry on paper towels.

COOKING METHODS

HALF-BOIL, HALF-STEAM METHOD

For up to 1½lb of green vegetables, pour ½ inch of boiling water into a pan. Put in the vegetables, cut up well, bring back to a boil, cover, and half-boil, half-steam for a few minutes until tender.

STIR-FRYING

A stainless steel wok is best for this technique, though a large frying pan can be used. Prepare the vegetables in advance, then heat a tablespoon of oil, such as peanut, until smoking hot. Add the vegetables and stir vigorously while they fry until they are heated through but still crisp: a few minutes.

BAIN-MARIE

When cooking a delicate dish, such as an egg-set terrine, set the baking dish in a large pan of very hot water and place in the oven with the temperature on low. This method works on the stove, too: set a bowl over a saucepan of simmering water to achieve the gentle heat required for making hollandaise sauce, melting chocolate, or keeping a dish of food warm.

STEAMING

Steaming is an excellent way of cooking small to medium-sized amounts of vegetables – with the exception of leafy green vegetables, which I think are best half-boiled, half-steamed (see left). A stainless steel steamer set over a saucepan is ideal: you can cook one vegetable in the steamer while another is half-boiling, half-steaming in the pan below, saving heat and space.

DEEP-FRYING

To fry a small quantity of food, it is best to use an ordinary saucepan, not a vast deep-fryer. For larger quantities you can also use a wok. Fill the pan no more than half-full with oil (less for a wok): both peanut and vegetable oils are suitable. The oil needs to be hot: 350°F/180°C. Use a candy thermometer, or dip the handle of a wooden spoon or a wooden chopstick into the oil – bubbles will instantly form around the spoon handle or chopstick if the oil is hot enough. Make sure the food is dry when you put it in to prevent splattering, retrieve it after cooking using a slotted spoon, and drain it well on crumpled paper towels. Ideally, replace oil after using it twice.

EGGS & MILK

Eggs and milk are useful and versatile ingredients. For instance, the air whisked into egg whites makes soufflés rise, while egg yolks make custards and terrines set. Milk is the basis for one of the most adaptable sauces, béchamel, while delicious crêpes and pancakes are made with milk, eggs, and flour. And of course, eggs on their own make the classically simple omelette.

BÉCHAMEL SAUCE

To make 1 cup of medium-thick sauce, use:

2 tbsps butter
¼ cup flour
1½ cups milk

MAKING THE ROUX

1 Melt the butter in a saucepan over moderate heat, then add the flour and stir until the flour is incorporated: 1–2 minutes.

ADDING THE MILK

2 Over the heat, pour in one-third of the milk and stir well; the mixture will go lumpy, then thick and smooth. Stir in another third of the milk, and then repeat with the final third.

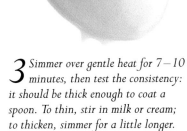

3 Simmer over gentle heat for 7–10 minutes, then test the consistency: it should be thick enough to coat a spoon. To thin, stir in milk or cream; to thicken, simmer for a little longer.

FOLDING AN OMELETTE

1 Cook the omelette gently until it begins to set, drawing the edges in with a fork. When the underside is set but the top is still creamy, loosen the edges with a spatula and fold over one-third.

2 Tip the pan and slide the omelette onto a warm plate. As it slides out, flip the folded section over again, using the spatula if necessary, so that the omelette is folded in three.

FILLED OMELETTES
This technique is usually used for filled omelettes. Place the filling in the center before folding in three. Sweet omelettes may be spread with jam before folding.

SEPARATING AN EGG

Make sure the bowl you use is completely grease-free. Crack the egg and then, holding it over the bowl, let the white run into the bowl. Transfer the yolk from one half of the shell to the other to allow more white to run into the bowl. Take care not to get even a speck of egg yolk in with the whites, or they won't whisk.

<table>
<tr><td>

TIPS FOR WHISKING EGG WHITES

• *A balloon whisk and copper bowl give the greatest volume. A rotary hand whisk or an electric whisk is also effective.*

• *Don't over-whisk; stop as soon as the whites stand up in soft peaks or they will collapse.*

</td></tr>
</table>

CREPE BATTER

Makes twelve 6-inch crêpes.

INGREDIENTS

1 cup whole-wheat flour
pinch of salt
2 eggs
1 tbsp olive oil or melted butter
1¼ cups milk

PREPARATION

FOOD PROCESSOR METHOD: Place all the ingredients in a food processsor or blender and blend until smooth.

HAND METHOD: Sift the flour and salt into a bowl. Make a well in the center and break in the eggs. Add the oil or butter. Stir the mixture with a wire whisk, then gradually add the milk, beating the batter until it is smooth.

Tossing pancakes on Shrove Tuesday is a long-standing tradition. Use the crêpe batter recipe above, but make the pancakes much thicker if you want to toss them.

PASTRY

Shortcrust and quick flaky pastry are not nearly as complicated to make as many people think. In fact it's easy and satisfying to make your own, and learning the basics will open up a whole repertoire of dishes. Phyllo pastry, bought ready-made, is also simple to use and can produce stunning results.

BASIC SHORTCRUST PASTRY

*Makes one 8-inch pastry shell
or four 4-inch individual shells,
or 8 or more tartlets, depending on their size.*

INGREDIENTS

*½ cup whole-wheat flour
½ cup all-purpose flour
¼ tsp salt
4 tbsps butter, cut into pieces
1 egg yolk, optional
1½−2 tbsps water*

PREPARATION

1 Sift the flours and salt into a large bowl, adding the bran left in the sieve.
2 Add the butter and rub it in with your fingertips or work briefly in a food processor until the mixture resembles bread crumbs.
3 Add the egg yolk if desired (it gives the pastry an extra light, crisp texture) and enough cold water to make a dough that leaves the edges of the bowl clean. Wrap in plastic wrap and chill in the refrigerator for 30 minutes.
4 Preheat the oven to 400°F/200°C.
5 Roll the pastry out thinly on a lightly floured board. To make individual pastry shells, divide the pastry into four and roll each one out separately. Whole-wheat pastry is more fragile than white because of the bran, so do not attempt to lift it. Use the board, as shown above right, to transfer the pastry into the pan.
6 Line and prepare the pan(s) as shown. Press the pastry gently into place, trim off surplus, and prick the base with a fork. To prevent the pastry from bubbling up while cooking, bake it blind: line the pastry shell with waxed paper or foil and weigh it down with dried beans.
7 Bake in the center of the preheated oven for 15 minutes, then remove the beans and paper and bake for 10 minutes longer, or until the pastry is crisp and golden brown.

QUICK FLAKY PASTRY

Makes one 8-inch pastry crust plus decorations.

INGREDIENTS

*1½ cups all-purpose flour
¼ tsp salt
8 tbsps cold butter
squeeze of lemon juice
small glass of ice water*

PREPARATION

1 Sift the flour and salt into a large bowl and place in the refrigerator or freezer to chill thoroughly: about 30 minutes. The colder the ingredients are for this pastry, the better.
2 Grate the butter into the flour, dipping it in flour if it becomes too sticky to grate.
3 Add a squeeze of lemon juice, then, mixing with a fork, stir in enough ice water to make a lumpy dough that just holds together and leaves the sides of the bowl clean.
4 Gather the dough up into a ball, wrap it in plastic wrap and chill for 30 minutes.
5 Preheat the oven to 400°F/200°C.
6 Roll the pastry out thinly on a lightly floured board and use as required.

USING PHYLLO PASTRY

• *Although you can make phyllo pastry at home, I really don't think it is worth it — some of the supermarket brands are exceptional. Recipes in this book are based on sheets of phyllo measuring approximately 13 x 8 inches.*

• *Brush a sheet of phyllo pastry with butter and place another sheet on top for a deliciously flaky effect. Don't brush if you prefer low-fat pastry.*

• *Phyllo pastry dries out and becomes brittle on contact with air, so remove one sheet at a time and keep the rest covered with plastic wrap or a damp dish cloth until needed.*

MAKING A PASTRY SHELL

Whole-wheat pastry is crumbly, so it helps to transfer it to the pan using a board. My method (see step 4) of "waterproofing" the pastry shell before adding the filling is unusual, but it helps to avoid soggy bases.

1 Leave the rolled-out pastry on the board, making sure it's not sticking. Hold the board over the far rim of the pan, then slide the pastry off the board into the pan.

2 Gently ease the pastry into the edges of the pan and press lightly but firmly into position.

3 Run a rolling pin over the pan to detach the excess pastry. Prick the base with a fork and line with waxed paper or foil and beans. Bake until crisp and lightly browned, removing paper and beans after 15 minutes.

4 Heat 2 tbsps vegetable oil in a small pan. As soon as it comes out of the oven, spoon the hot oil over the hot pastry: it will sizzle, fry the surface of the pastry, and "waterproof" it.

PIE PREPARATION

Use a pie dish, and heap up the filling in the center to give the pie an attractive domed shape. Make sure the filling has completely cooled before you cover it, or the flaky pastry may start to melt.

1 To make the edge of the pie rise in flakes, cut into it with the back of a knife. Then scallop the pie by going around the edge with your finger and the back of a knife as shown.

2 Cut diamond shapes from a strip of leftover pastry, and score with the back of the knife to make "leaf veins." Arrange on top of the pie, brushing with water or milk to seal.

3 To glaze, brush the pie with milk or beaten egg mixed with ½ tsp salt (the salt helps to make the glaze shiny). Cut a vent for the steam to escape.

You can decorate the pie with a variety of shapes. Little cookie cutters are useful for hearts, stars, and other shapes.

GRAINS, LEGUMES, & SPICES

Rice, millet, and other grains, dried beans, lentils, nuts, and seeds are all wonderfully nutritious, providing a healthy source of protein in the vegetarian diet. The many varieties of grain require fairly similar preparation, so once the principles are understood there is room to experiment. Nuts and seeds can be prepared, too: toasted to enhance their flavor or ground to alter their texture.

COOKING RICE

Many varieties of rice are widely available. My staple is long-grain brown rice, but I also like long-grain white rice and I love the delicate fragrance of basmati rice, both brown and white. For risottos I use Italian arborio rice: other varieties don't give the same creamy result. Various types of glutinous short-grain or "sticky" rice, whose grains cling together, are also available. Wild rice (not really a grain but a grass) is delicious mixed with other kinds of rice.

ABSORPTION METHOD

A useful method for the busy cook: allow 1 measure of rice to 2 of water or 1 cup to 2 cups. Put in a pan and bring to a boil. Cover tightly, turn the heat down to low, and cook until the rice is tender and the water absorbed (see times opposite). Remove from the heat and keep covered for 5 – 10 minutes longer. Fluff up the rice with a fork.

DRAINING METHOD

Bring 10 cups of water to a boil in a large saucepan. Add 1 cup of rice and stir. Cook until the rice is tender: 12 minutes for long-grain white rice, 20–25 minutes for brown, around 10 for white basmati, 15 for brown. Drain, rinse under hot water, drain again, and spoon into a warmed dish with seasoning and, if desired, a little butter.

SHORT-GRAIN RICE

Glutinous short-grain rice is often used in Thai, Chinese, and Japanese cooking. Because of its high starch content the grains tend to clump together, instead of being fluffy and separate. This makes it ideal for Eastern dishes, as it is easy to pick up sticky rice with chopsticks. This rice is used for both sweet and savory dishes. Cook by the absorption method (see above).

RICE COOKING TIMES

These cooking times are for the absorption method of cooking rice and are based on 1 cup of rice and 2 cups of water – allow fractionally less water for basmati rice and fractionally more for brown rice (up to 2¼ cups). You can also add some salt, though rice is a food that I prefer unsalted. Rinse basmati rice before cooking by swirling it in a large bowl of water, then drain. Repeat 2 – 3 times: this gives a lighter result.

Long-grain white rice *15 – 20 minutes*

Long-grain brown rice *40 – 45 minutes*

White basmati rice *10 – 15 minutes*

Brown basmati rice *15 – 20 minutes*

Glutinous short-grain rice *20 minutes*

Wild rice *45 minutes*

COUSCOUS AND BULGUR

The easiest way to cook these grains is to put one tablespoon of oil into a large saucepan with 1½ cups of water and 1½ teaspoons of salt. Bring to a boil, then add 8oz of couscous or bulgur. Remove from the heat and leave to swell: 2 minutes for couscous, 10 for bulgur. Add a little butter and heat gently, stirring with a fork, until heated through: about 3 minutes.

PREPARING DRIED BEANS

Cover beans with cold water and soak for 8 – 12 hours. Drain, rinse, then place in pan and cover with their height again in cold water. Boil rapidly for 10 minutes, then reduce the heat and simmer until tender: 1 – 1½ hours for most beans.

SEEDS AND SPICES

Many seeds make wonderful flavorings. They range from the aromatics, such as sesame and fennel, to the spicy-flavored, such as cumin, cardamom, and coriander, often used in Eastern and Indian cooking.

DRY-FRYING SPICES

To bring out their flavor, crush spices before use, and heat them in a dry pan for a few minutes. Cumin, coriander, fennel, and cardamom seeds respond particularly well. Sesame seeds are delicious toasted lightly in a dry pan or under a hot broiler, but watch them in case they burn.

Cumin   **Sesame**

PREPARING STAR ANISE

You can use star anise whole, or you can break off the points of the "star" and crush them lightly with your fingers to free the shiny seeds. Use these seeds whole or lightly crushed.

PREPARING CARDAMOM

Bruise cardamom pods in a mortar and then add to spicy dishes; or crush to loosen the outer casings, then remove these and crush the remaining tiny seeds to a powder.

GRATING GINGER

Wash but don't bother to peel the ginger – the peel comes away easily as you grate. To prepare ginger for cooking, use the small holes (but not the very smallest) on a flat or box grater.

GROUND SEEDS FOR SPICE

Many seeds used as spices – such as coriander and cumin – can be bought in ground form. Since ground spices quickly lose their aroma, check your pantry regularly and throw away those that have lost their fragrance. Buy ground spices in small quantities and use them quickly, or grind the spices yourself to ensure freshness.

TOASTING NUTS AND SEEDS

Spread the nuts or seeds on the broiler pan or on a baking sheet. Broil for a few minutes or bake at 350°F/180°C until golden brown. Keep an eye on them; some nuts toast quickly. Use at once or store in an airtight container for a few days.

THE VEGETARIAN PANTRY

Classic vegetarian cooking does not demand strange ingredients that are difficult to obtain: most are widely available. Buy the best quality you can and store them carefully, as described.

Keeping the basics on hand means you can always put a simple meal together. To store herbs and spices, I prefer open shelves to cupboards: seeing them gives me inspiration while I work.

•

THE PANTRY

A cool, dry, airy cupboard is ideal for most non-perishable foods. Keep some of these in stock and you'll save a great deal of time and be able to put together quick meals at short notice. It's best to buy flours, grains, and legumes in small quantities and keep them in airtight jars, or wrap in a plastic bag once opened.

FRUIT & VEGETABLES
Most fruit and vegetables are best kept in the refrigerator; those for the pantry include dried fruits such as apricots and raisins; citrus fruits, apples, and bananas; unripe avocados and mangoes (once ripe put them in the refrigerator); onions, garlic, and potatoes.

FRESH HERBS
Herbs in pots can be kept on a windowsill until used up.

FLAVORINGS
All of the following are useful to keep in stock:
• Sea salt: I like the light flaky kind that crumbles in your fingers.
• Black peppercorns in a grinder.
• Red and white wine vinegars, rice and balsamic vinegars.
• Soy sauce: good quality, made without coloring or caramel.
• Jar of light tahini or sesame seed paste (stir before use).
• Honeys of different types.
• Dried porcini mushrooms.
• Vegetable stock cubes.
• Stem ginger in syrup.

SPICES
Buy in small quantities so that you can use them up while they're fresh and fragrant. I keep mine lined up in alphabetical order on long shelves over my work surface.

OILS
These are the oils I keep in stock:
• Light olive oil, perfect for all basic cooking. I also keep a bottle of the best olive oil I can afford, which I use in salads.
• Peanut oil for deep-frying.
• Toasted sesame oil for fragrant and flavorful stir-fries.
• Walnut oil for salads – expensive but a treat.

CANNED FOODS
I keep these cans in stock:
• Artichoke hearts in brine.
• Whole plum tomatoes in juice.
• Various beans and lentils: whole green lentils, red kidney beans, chickpeas, and cannellini beans are all useful.
• Bamboo shoots and straw mushrooms for Chinese-style stir-fries.

PACKAGED FOODS
These are good to keep on hand but remember that most don't last indefinitely, so they should be sorted regularly. All of the following are essential:
• Various shapes of dried pasta.
• White and whole-wheat flour; also cornstarch or potato flour.
• Bulgur, couscous, and polenta.
• Long-grain and basmati rice, both brown and white; plus arborio rice for risottos.
• Split red lentils.
• Brown sugar; superfine sugar with a vanilla bean buried in it.

USEFUL SPICES

Bay leaves
Cardamom pods
*Cayenne pepper **or** chili powder*
Cinnamon powder
Cinnamon sticks
Cloves, whole and ground
Coriander, whole and ground
Cumin, whole and ground
Fennel seeds
Garam masala
Ginger, ground
Mustard powder
Mustard seeds
Nutmeg, whole
Paprika
Saffron
Star anise
Turmeric, ground

THE REFRIGERATOR

I recommend any vegetarian or would-be vegetarian buying a new refrigerator to get the biggest one possible because the refrigerator is such a good place to store fruit and vegetables, and having a spacious one means being able to store enough for up to a week at a time. It is also the place, of course, for dairy foods.

VEGETABLES

All of the following keep best in the refrigerator: all green leafy vegetables, all root vegetables except potatoes and sweet potatoes, green beans, snow peas, fresh mushrooms, zucchini, eggplants, peppers, bean sprouts, fresh baby corn cobs, scallions, asparagus, leeks, fennel, tomatoes, celery, cucumber, cauliflower, broccoli, and pumpkin once it's been cut.

FRUIT

Once fully ripened, delicate fruits keep longer if stored in the refrigerator: figs, apricots, peaches, pears, mango, papaya, star fruit, plums, cherries, and melon once it's been cut.

FRESH HERBS

Packages of fresh herbs go into the refrigerator but bunches of fresh cilantro and flat-leaf parsley keep well – and look attractive – standing in a pitcher of water on a kitchen shelf.

EGGS

Free-range eggs, preferably from a small producer, are the only kind I ever use and I keep them in the refrigerator.

CHEESE

Cheddar, Parmesan, and Gruyère are the basics that I always keep, carefully wrapped, in the refrigerator. At other times I may have Brie, a goat cheese log, Camembert, feta, mozzarella (packed in water), blue cheese, and soft white cheese ranging from low-fat versions to cottage cheese, cream cheese (especially the type flavored with herbs and garlic), and mascarpone. Vegetarian cheeses (made with vegetarian rennet) are often available: if this information is not given on the package, do ask.

MILK, YOGURT, & CREAM

I buy milk, yogurt, and cream – light, whipping, heavy, sour, or crème fraîche – in small quantities as and when needed.

FATS

Salted and unsalted butter are my basics. For vegan dishes I use unhydrogenated margarine. I also store creamed coconut to use in curries; it keeps well.

FLAVORINGS

All of these are useful: fresh ginger, olives, sundried tomatoes and sundried tomato paste, tubes of tomato purée once opened, lemongrass, fresh chilis, mustard including Dijon, capers in salt, and creamed horseradish.

THE FREEZER

The freezer is handy for keeping a supply of certain ingredients, such as fruit, vegetables, and pastry, and is very useful for emergencies. If I have a big event to cook for, like a holiday dinner, I make some dishes in advance and freeze them, but on the whole I prefer to make dishes fresh when they're needed.

FRUIT & VEGETABLES

Corn cobs, peas, broad beans, and leaf spinach; and some frozen raspberries for a treat.

NUTS

If you buy large quantities, keep them in the freezer to stop them from going rancid. You can use them straight from the freezer.

PASTRY

Frozen puff and phyllo pastry are useful. Refreeze unused phyllo.

OTHER FOODS

Small containers of frozen cream are useful for when just a little cream is needed for a recipe. And if I have an abundance of stock, I freeze it in small batches.

FOOD TO FREEZE

• *Pastry quiche shells, either cooked or ready for cooking.*

• *Crêpes, ready for stuffing or serving with sugar and lemon.*

• *One or two vegetarian savory dishes that are quick to reheat, such as small twice-baked soufflés, miniature quiches, and lasagna made in individual portions.*

• *Packages of phyllo pastry, both unopened and resealed. Wrap the pastry in plastic wrap before resealing.*

NOTES ON EQUIPMENT

BAKING PANS

Aim to collect a wide range of strong pans: they will last a lifetime if chosen carefully. Most useful are two sizes of 1lb loaf pan: one 3 inches deep, and a shallower one, 2 inches deep. A small jelly roll pan measuring 7 x 11 inches and a medium-sized one measuring 10 x 14 inches are also worth having. A strong baking pan with shallow sides is best for roasting vegetables and can double as a baking sheet. Pie pans of various sizes are useful: I like an 8-inch round one with a removable base for most kinds of quiche. For small individual quiches, I use 4-inch pans with shallow sides of about ¾ inch. A dozen tiny barquette pans are perfect for tartlets; for a big batch, remove the pastry shells when cooled and re-use the pans. Also useful are an 8-inch springclip pan, an 8-inch square baking pan and a bun or muffin pan with 12 sections.

FRYING PANS

I don't use anything other than nonstick frying pans. A frying pan measuring about 11 inches across the top is useful for general frying. Ideally you should also have a special omelette pan (with rounded sides) and a crêpe pan (with straight, shallow sides), each measuring about 6 inches across the base. In fact, I use an omelette pan for both.

CASSEROLES & DISHES

Rectangular baking dishes about 2 inches deep, measuring around 7½ x 11½ inches and 9½ x 13 inches are essential for such dishes as lasagna (in the larger dish) and gratin dauphinois (the smaller dish). Other useful items are small custard cups and timbale molds, straight-sided soufflé dishes, a big oval serving dish, and ovenproof pizza plates.

SAUCEPANS

Gradually build up a collection of good, strong saucepans in different sizes. I like good quality stainless steel. I also have a stainless-steel pressure cooker which I often use for soup because it is so quick.

WOK

I use a wok not only for stir-frying but also for deep-frying: the surface area of oil in a wok is greater than the surface area of the same amount of oil in a straight-sided pan. This means using less oil, and so it is not so extravagant to change it often. I use a stainless steel wok with a heatproof handle.

FOOD PROCESSOR / BLENDER

Although you can cook vegetarian food without one, a food processor opens up a whole new range of possibilities. Buy an easy-to-assemble model that does all the basics – chopping, grating, and slicing – so you do not need to spend money on extras. A large-capacity one that will process soups easily is also a good idea. A blender is useful for soups and purées but is not nearly as versatile as a food processor.

CUTTING BOARD

This is my most vital piece of equipment, along with my two favorite sharp knives and my potato peeler. I use a thick, strong wooden board not less than 12 x 16 inches; some people prefer firm white plastic. Either type doubles as a pastry board.

GRATER

A box grater that you can stand on the cutting board is just right for grating small quantities of cheese or vegetables. I also use a small hand-held rotary grater with different-sized drums and a small nutmeg grater with a compartment for storing the nutmeg.

KITCHEN SCISSORS

Scissors make quick work of many jobs such as snipping fresh herbs and trimming phyllo pastry.

KNIVES

The essential knife is a traditional, good quality French chef's knife with a 5-inch blade. Buy an expensive one and it will last for years; hold it first to check the balance before you buy it. You'll also need a steel for sharpening the knife. Second most essential in my opinion is a knife with a 5-inch serrated, stainless steel blade.

MORTAR & PESTLE

Not essential but useful for crushing spices. Choose a heavy ceramic one with a reasonably sized mortar; it works best when the mortar is less than half-full.

POTATO PEELER

A sharp, swivel-bladed potato peeler is an essential piece of equipment; I prefer a peeler with a long, comfortable handle (many are far too short).

ROLLING PIN

Useful if you like making pastry, although improvised substitutes are possible, such as a wine bottle. I prefer a long wooden rolling pin without handles.

WHISK

For years I put off buying a hand-held electric whisk but when I eventually bought one (on sale) I couldn't believe how useful it was. Now I consider it one of my most vital pieces of equipment – and it's relatively cheap. Choose a lightweight one with a switch that's easy to operate.

INDEX

ACKNOWLEDGMENTS

Author's appreciation
I would like to thank everyone involved in producing this book for their inspiration, care, and attention to detail and for making the whole process such a pleasure. My warmest thanks and appreciation firstly to Christopher Davis and Daphne Razazan for being so enthusiastic from the beginning; and to Rosie Pearson and Carole Ash; to my wonderful editor and art editor, Mari Roberts and Tracey Clarke, with whom I so much enjoyed working; to the photographers Amanda Heywood and Clive Streeter, for taking so much trouble and making the photo sessions so pleasant; to all the talented food stylists,

particularly Lyn Rutherford, for preparing the recipes so well for the photographs; to my agent Barbara Levy; to my daughter Claire for tasting and fun, and most especially my husband Robert for support, (more!) tasting, and living with all that writing a book entails.

Dorling Kindersley would like to thank Alexa Stace and Lorna Damms for editorial help; Lyn Rutherford, Kathy Man, Carole Handslip, and Jill Eggleton for preparing the food that appears throughout the book; Sarah Ponder for the artworks; Sarah Ereira for the index, and Artemi Kyriacou for photographic assistance.